Community

THEMES FOR THE 21ST CENTURY

Titles in this series

Forthcoming

Community

Seeking Safety in an Insecure World

ZYGMUNT BAUMAN

Polity

First published in 2001 by Polity Press in association with Blackwell Publishing Ltd

Reprinted 2001, 2002, 2003, 2004 (twice), 2006, 2007

Polity Press
65 Bridge Street
Cambridge CB2 1UR, UK

Polity Press
350 Main Street
Malden, MA 02148, USA

ISBN 978-0-7456-2634-5
ISBN 978-0-7456-2635-2 (pbk)

A catalogue record for this book is available from the British Library and has been applied for from the Library of Congress.

Typeset in 10.5 on 12 pt Plantin by SetSystems Ltd, Saffron Walden, Essex
Printed in United States by Odyssey Press Inc., Gonic, New Hampshire
This book is printed on acid-free paper.
For further information on Polity, visit our website :http://www.polity.co.uk

Contents

An Overture, or Welcome to Elusive Community

Words have meanings: some words, however, also have a 'feel'. The word 'community' is one of them. It feels good: whatever the word 'community' may mean, it is good 'to have a community', 'to be in a community'. If someone wandered off the right track, we would often explain his unwholesome conduct by saying that 'he has fallen into bad *company*.' If someone is miserable, suffers a lot and is consistently denied a dignified life, we promptly accuse *society* – the way it is organized, the way it works. Company or society can be bad; but not the *community*. Community, we feel, is always a good thing.

The meanings and feelings the words convey are not, of course, independent of each other. 'Community' feels good because of the meanings the word 'community' conveys – all of them promising pleasures, and more often than not the kinds of pleasures we would like to experience but seem to miss.

To start with, community is a 'warm' place, a cosy and comfortable place. It is like a roof under which we shelter in heavy rain, like a fireplace at which we warm our hands on a frosty day. Out there, in the street, all sorts of dangers lie in ambush; we have to be alert when we go out, watch whom we are talking to and who talks to us, be on the look-out every minute. In here, in the community, we can relax – we are safe, there are no dangers looming in dark corners (to be sure, hardly any 'corner' here is 'dark'). In a community, we all understand each other well, we may trust what we hear, we are safe most of the time and hardly ever puzzled or taken aback. We are never strangers to each other. We may quarrel – but these are friendly quarrels, it is just that we are all trying to make our togetherness even better and more enjoyable than it has been so far and, while guided by the same wish to improve our life together, we may disagree how to do it best. But we never wish each other bad luck, and we may be sure that all the others around wish us good.

To go on: in a community we can count on each other's good will. If we stumble and fall, others will help us to stand on our feet again. No one will poke fun at us, no one will ridicule our clumsiness and rejoice in our misfortune. If we do take a wrong step, we can still confess, explain and apologize, repent if necessary; people will listen with sympathy and forgive us so that no one will hold a grudge forever. And there will always be someone to hold our hand at moments of sadness. When we fall on hard times and we are genuinely in need, people won't ask us for collateral before deciding to bail us out of trouble; they won't be asking us how and when will we repay, but what our needs are. And they will hardly ever say that helping us is not their duty and refuse to help us because there is no contract between us obliging them to do so, or because we failed to read the small print of the contract properly. Our duty, purely and simply, is to help each other, and so our right, purely and simply, is to expect that the help we need will be forthcoming.

And so it is easy to see why the word 'community' feels good. Who would not wish to live among friendly and well-wishing people whom one could trust and on whose words and deeds one could rely? For us in particular –

who happen to live in ruthless times, times of competition and one-upmanship, when people around seem to keep their cards close to their chests and few people seem to be in any hurry to help us, when in reply to our cries for help we hear admonitions to help ourselves, when only the banks eager to mortgage our possessions are smiling and wishing to say 'yes', and even they only in their commercials, not in their branch offices – the word 'community' sounds sweet. What that word evokes is everything we miss and what we lack to be secure, confident and trusting.

In short, 'community' stands for the kind of world which is not, regrettably, available to us – but which we would dearly wish to inhabit and which we hope to repossess. Raymond Williams, the thoughtful analyst of our shared condition, observed caustically that the remarkable thing about community is that 'it always has been'. We may add: or that it is always in the future. 'Community' is nowadays another name for paradise lost – but one to which we dearly hope to return, and so we feverishly seek the roads that may bring us there.

Paradise lost or a paradise still hoped to be found; one way or another, this is definitely not a paradise that we inhabit and not the paradise that we know from our own experience. Perhaps it is a paradise precisely for these reasons. Imagination, unlike the harsh realities of life, is an expanse of unbridled freedom. Imagination we can 'let loose', and we do, with impunity – since we have not much chance of putting what we have imagined to the test of life.

It is not just the 'harsh reality', the admittedly 'noncommunal' or even the explicitly community-hostile reality, that differs from that imagined community with a 'warm feel'. That difference, if anything, only spurs our imagination to run faster and makes the imagined com-

munity even more alluring. On this difference, the imagined (postulated, dreamed of) community feeds and
thrives. What spells trouble for the cloudless image is
another difference: that between the community of our
dreams and the 'really existing community': a collectivity
which pretends to be community incarnate, the dream
fulfilled, and (in the name of all the goodness such
community is assumed to offer) demands unconditional
loyalty and treats everything short of such loyalty as an act
of unforgivable treason. The 'really existing community',
were we to find ourselves in its grasp, would demand
stern obedience in exchange for the services it renders or
promises to render. Do you want security? Give up your
freedom, or at least a good chunk of it. Do you want
confidence? Do not trust anybody outside your community. Do you want mutual understanding? Don't speak
to foreigners nor use foreign languages. Do you want this
cosy home feeling? Fix alarms on your door and TV
cameras on your drive. Do you want safety? Do not let
the strangers in and yourself abstain from acting strangely
and thinking odd thoughts. Do you want warmth? Do not
come near the window, and never open one. The snag is
that if you follow this advice and keep the windows sealed,
the air inside would soon get stuffy and in the end
oppressive.

There is a price to be paid for the privilege of 'being in
a community' – and it is inoffensive or even invisible only
as long as the community stays in the dream. The price is
paid in the currency of freedom, variously called 'autonomy', 'right to self-assertion', 'right to be yourself'. Whatever you choose, you gain some and lose some. Missing
community means missing security; gaining community,
if it happens, would soon mean missing freedom. Security
and freedom are two equally precious and coveted values
which could be better or worse balanced, but hardly ever

fully reconciled and without friction. At any rate, no foolproof recipe for such reconciliation has yet been invented. The problem is that the recipe from which the 'really existing communities' are made only renders the contradiction between security and freedom more obtrusive and harder to repair.

Given the unsavoury attributes with which freedom without security is burdened, as much as is security without freedom, it looks as if we will never stop dreaming of a community, but neither will we ever find in any self-proclaimed community the pleasures we savoured in our dreams. The argument between security and freedom, and so the argument between community and individuality, is unlikely ever to be resolved and so likely to go on for a long time to come; not finding the right solution and being frustrated by the one that has been tried will not prompt us to abandon the search – but to go on trying. Being human, we can neither fulfil the hope nor cease hoping.

There is little we can do to escape the dilemma – we can deny it only at our peril. One good thing we can do, however, is to take stock of the chances and the dangers which solutions proposed and tried have in store. Armed with such knowledge, we may at least avoid repeating past errors; we may also avoid hazarding ourselves too far along the roads which can be known in advance to be blind alleys. It is such a taking of stock – admittedly provisional and far from complete – that I've attempted in this book.

We cannot be human without both security and freedom; but we cannot have both at the same time and both in quantities which we find fully satisfactory. This is not a reason to stop trying (we would not stop anyway, even if it was). But it is a reminder that we should never believe that any of the successive interim solutions needs no

further scrutiny or could not benefit from another correction. The better may be an enemy of the good, but most
certainly the 'perfect' is a mortal enemy of both.

March 2000

1

The Agony of Tantalus

According to Greek mythology, Tantalus – son of Zeus and Pluto, was on excellent terms with the gods who frequently invited him to wine and dine in their company at Olympic feasts. His life was, by ordinary folks' standards, trouble-free, joyful and all together happy – until, that is, he committed a crime which gods would not (could not?) forgive. As for the nature of that crime, various tellers of the story differ. Some say that he abused divine trust by betraying to his fellow-men the mysteries meant to be kept secret from the mortals. Others say that he was arrogant enough to suspect himself wiser than the gods and resolved to put the divine power of observation to the test. Other story-tellers still charged Tantalus with the theft of nectar and ambrosia which mortal creatures were not meant to taste. The acts imputed to Tantalus were, as we can see, different, but the reason for which they had been declared criminal was much the same in all three cases: Tantalus was guilty of acquiring/sharing knowledge which neither he nor other mortals like him should have. Or, more to the point: Tantalus would not stop at the partaking of divine bliss: in his conceit and arrogance he wished to make for himself what could be enjoyed only as a gift.

The punishment was swift; it was also as cruel as only

offended and vengeful gods could make it. Given the nature of Tantalus' crime, it was an object-lesson. Tantalus was stood up to his neck in a stream – but when he lowered his head wishing to quench his thirst, the water flew away. Over his head hung a luscious bunch of fruit – but whenever he stretched out a hand wishing to satiate his hunger, a sudden gust of wind blew the appetizing titbits away. (Hence, whenever things tend to vanish the moment we seem to have got them, at long last, within our reach – we complain of being 'tantalized' by their 'tantalizing' nearness.)

Myths do not tell stories to amuse. They are meant to teach, by endlessly reiterating their message: a kind of message which listeners may forget or neglect only at their peril. The message of the Tantalus myth is that you may stay happy, or at least stay happy blissfully and without worry, only as long as you keep your innocence: as long as you just enjoy your happiness while staying ignorant of the nature of the things that made you happy and not try to tinker with them, let alone to take them 'into your own hands'. And that if you do dare to take matters into your own hands you will never resurrect the bliss which you could enjoy only in the state of innocence. Your goal will forever escape your grasp.

Other peoples than the Greeks must also have arrived at believing in the eternal truth and perpetual topicality of that message as they drew on their own experience; the Greeks were not alone in including that message among the stories they told to teach, and listened to learn. A very similar message flows from the story of Adam and Eve, whose penalty for eating from the Tree of Knowledge was expulsion from paradise; and the paradise was a paradise because they could live there trouble-free: they did not have to make the choices on which their happiness (or for that matter unhappiness) depended. The Jewish God could be on occasion no less cruel and unforgiving in his wrath than the residents of Olympus, and the penalty he designed to punish Adam's and Eve's offence was no less painful than the lot visited on Tantalus – it was only, so to speak, more sophisticated and called for more interpretative skills: 'With labour you shall win your food . . . You shall gain your bread by the sweat of your brow.' While announcing this verdict, an angry God stationed 'to the east of the Garden of Eden' 'the cherubim and a sword whirling and flashing to guard the way to the tree of life' – to warn Adam and Eve and their offspring that no amount of labour or sweating would suffice to bring back the serene and carefree happiness of paradise ignorance; that happiness of the pristine sort had been irretrievably lost once innocence was lost.

Memory of that bliss would haunt Adam's and Eve's descendants and keep them hoping against hope that the road back could be discovered or blazed. This is, though, not to be – ever; on this point there was no disagreement between Athens and Jerusalem. Loss of innocence is a point of no return. One can be truly happy only as long as one does not know how truly happy one is. Having learned the meaning of happiness through its loss, children of Adam and Eve were bound to learn the hard way the bitter wisdom which to Tantalus was delivered on a platter. Their purpose would always elude them, however close (*tantalizingly* close) it might seem to be.

In the book which (intentionally or not) invited 'community' (*Gemeinschaft*) to return from the exile to which it had been banished during the modern crusade against *les pouvoirs intermédiaires* (accused of parochiality, narrowness of horizons and nurturing of superstition), Ferdinand Tönnies[1] suggested that what distinguished the bygone community from the rising (modern) society (*Gesellschaft*) in whose name the crusade was launched, was an *understanding shared by all its members*. Not a consensus, mind you: consensus is but an agreement reached by essentially differently minded people, a product of hard negotiation and compromise, of a lot of bickering, much contrariness, and occasional fisticuffs. The community-style, matter-of-factly (*zuhanden*, as Martin Heidegger would say) understanding does not need to be sought, let alone laboriously *built* or *fought for*: that understanding 'is there', ready-made and ready to use – so that we understand each other 'without words' and never need to ask, apprehensively, 'what do you mean?' The kind of understanding on which community rests *precedes* all agreements and disagreements. Such understanding is not a finishing line, but the *starting point* of all togetherness. It is a 'reciprocal, binding sentiment' – 'the proper and real will of those bound together'; and it is thanks to such understanding, and such understanding only, that in community people 'remain essentially united in spite of all separating factors'.

Many years after Tönnies singled out 'common understanding' 'coming naturally' as the feature which sets the community apart from the world of bitter quarrels, cutthroat competition, horse-trading and log-rolling, Göran Rosenberg, the perceptive Swedish analyst, coined the concept of the 'warm circle' (in an essay in 2000 in *La Nouvelle Lettre Internationale*), to grasp the same kind of naive immersion in human togetherness – once perhaps a common human condition, but nowadays available, increasingly, only in dreams. Human loyalties, offered and matter-of-factly expected inside the 'warm circle', 'are not derived from external social logic, or from any economic cost-benefit analysis'. This is exactly what makes that circle 'warm': it has no room for cold calculation and rota-learning of whatever society around, frostily and humourlessly, presents as 'standing to reason'. And this is exactly why frost-bitten people dream of that magic circle and would wish to cut that other, cold world to its size and measure. Inside the 'warm circle' they won't have to prove anything, and whatever they do they may expect sympathy and help.

Because of being so self-evident and 'natural', the shared understanding which makes community (or, for that matter, the 'warm circle') escapes notice (we hardly ever notice the air we breathe, unless it is the foul and malodorous air of a stuffy room that we happen to inhale); it is, as Tönnies puts it, 'tacit' (or 'intuitive', in Rosenberg's terms). Of course, a contrived, an *achieved* understanding may also be tacit, or turn into a sort of contrived and internalized intuition. Protracted negotiation may result in an agreement which, if obeyed daily, may in its turn become a habit which no longer needs to be thought about, let alone monitored and policed. But unlike such sediments of past trials and tribulations, that sharing of understanding which is characteristic of a community is tacit 'according to its very nature':

> This is because the contents of mutual understanding are inexpressible, interminable, and incomprehensible . . . [R]eal concord cannot be artificially produced.

Since 'community' means shared understanding of the 'natural' and 'tacit' kind, it won't survive the moment in which understanding turns self-conscious, and so loud and vociferous; when, to use Heidegger's terminology again, understanding passes from the state of being 'zuhanden' to being 'vorhanden' and becomes an object for contemplation and scrutiny. Community can only be numb – or dead. Once it starts to praise its unique valour, wax lyrical about its pristine beauty and stick on nearby fences wordy manifestoes calling its members to appreciate its wonders and telling all the others to admire them or shut up – one can be sure that the community is no more (or not yet, as the case may be). 'Spoken of' community (more exactly: a community speaking of itself) is a contradiction in terms.

Not that real community, such as has not been 'artificially produced' or merely imagined, would have much chance of falling into that contradiction. Robert Redfield[2] would agree with Tönnies that in a true community there is no motivation towards reflection, criticism or experimentation; but, he would hurry to explain, this is the case because community is true to its nature (or to its ideal model) only in as far as it is *distinctive* from other human groupings (it is apparent 'where the community begins and where it ends'), *small* (so small as to be all within view of all its members), and *self-sufficient* (so that, as Redfield insists, it 'provides for all or more of the activities and needs of the people in it. The little community is a cradle-to-the-grave arrangement').

Redfield's choice of attributes is anything but random. 'Distinctiveness' means: the division into 'us' and 'them' is exhaustive as much as it is disjunctive, there are no 'betwixt and between' cases left, it is crystal-clear who is 'one of us' and who is not, there is no muddle and no cause for confusion – no cognitive ambiguity, and so no behavioural ambivalence. 'Smallness' means: communication among the insiders is all-embracing and dense, and so casts the signals sporadically arriving 'from the outside' into disadvantage by reason of their comparative rarity, superficiality and perfunctory character. While 'self-sufficiency' means: isolation from 'them' is close to complete, the occasions to break it are few and far between. All three features join forces in effectively protecting the members of the community from challenges to their habitual ways. As long as each and every one of the triune traits stays intact, it is indeed highly unlikely that the motivation to reflection, criticism and experimentation would ever arise.

As long as . . . Indeed, the pristine unity of the Redfield 'little community' depends on blocking the channels of communication with the rest of the inhabited world. The unity of community, as Redfield would say, or the 'naturalness' of communal understanding, as Tönnies would prefer to call it, are both made of the same stuff: of homogeneity, of *sameness*.

The sameness finds itself in trouble the moment its conditions begin to crumble: when the balance between 'inside' and 'outside' communication, once skewed sharply towards the interior, gets more even, thereby blurring the distinction between 'us' and 'them'. The sameness evaporates once the communication between its insiders and the world outside becomes more intense and carries more weight than the mutual exchanges of the insiders.

Precisely such a breach in the protective walls of community became a foregone conclusion with the appearance of mechanical means of transportation; carriers of alternative information (or people whose very strangeness was information distinct from, and clashing with, the knowledge internally available) could now in principle travel as quickly or faster than the word-of-mouth messages originating and circulated within the circumference of 'natural' human mobility. Distance, once the most formidable among the communal defences, lost much of its significance. The mortal blow to the 'naturalness' of communal understanding was delivered, however, by the advent of informatics: the emancipation of the flow of information from the transport of bodies. Once information could travel independently of its carriers, and with a speed far beyond the capacity of even the most advanced means of transportation (as in the kind of society we all nowadays inhabit), the boundary between 'inside' and 'outside' could no longer be drawn, let alone sustained.

From now on, all homogeneity must be 'hand-picked' from a tangled mass of variety through selection, separation and exclusion; all unity needs to be *made*; concord 'artificially produced' is the sole form of unity available. Common understanding can be only an *achievement*, attained (if at all) at the end of a long and tortuous labour of argument and persuasion and in strenous competition with an indefinite number of other potentialities – all vying for attention and each promising a better (more correct, more effective or more pleasurable) assortment of life tasks and solutions for life problems. And if reached, common agreement will be never free of the memory of such past struggles and the choices made in their course. However firmly it holds, therefore, no agreement will appear as 'natural' and as 'self-evident' as in the communities of Tönnies or Redfield, whatever its spokespeople and promoters do to portray it as such. It will be never immune from further reflection, contest and argument; if anything, it may reach the status of a 'rolling contract', an agreement to agree which needs to be periodically renewed, without any renewal carrying a guarantee of a next one.

Community of common understanding, even if reached, will therefore stay fragile and vulnerable, forever in need of vigilance, fortification and defence. People who dream of community in the hope of finding a long-term security which they miss so painfully in their daily pursuits, and of liberating themselves from the irksome burden of ever new and always risky choices, will be sorely disappointed. Peace of mind, if they find it, will prove to be of the 'until further notice' kind. Rather than an island of 'natural understanding', a 'warm circle' where they can lay down their arms and stop fighting, the *really existing*

community will feel like a besieged fortress being contin-
uously bombarded by (often invisible) enemies outside
while time and again being torn apart by discord within;
ramparts and turrets will be the places where the seekers
of communal warmth, homeliness and tranquillity will
have to spend most of their time.

This seems to be an observation common to the point
of triviality: once 'unmade', a community cannot be,
unlike the phoenix with its magical capacity of rising from
the ashes, put together again. If it does arise, it won't be
in the form preserved in memory (more precisely, con-
jured up by an imagination whipped up daily by perpetual
insecurity) – the only form that makes it look so desirable
as a better-than-any-other wholesale solution to all earthly
troubles. All this seems pretty obvious, but logic and
human dreams seldom if ever walk the same roads. And
there are good reasons, as we will see later, for their roads
never to converge for long.

As Eric Hobsbawm recently observed, 'never was the
word "community" used more indiscriminately and emp-
tily than in the decades when communities in the sociological sense became hard to find in real life';[3] and he
commented, 'Men and women look for groups to which
they can belong, certainly and forever, in a world in which
all else is moving and shifting, in which nothing else is
certain.'[4] Jock Young supplied a succinct and poignant
gloss on Hobsbawm's observation and commentary: 'Just
as community collapses, identity is invented.'[5]

'Identity', today's talk of the town and the most commonly played game in town, owes the attention it attracts
and the passions it begets to being a *surrogate of community*: of that allegedly 'natural home' or that circle that
stays warm however cold the winds outside. Neither of
the two is available in our rapidly privatized and individualized, fast globalizing world, and for that reason each of

the two can be safely, with no fear of practical test, imagined as a cosy shelter of security and confidence and for that reason hotly desired. The paradox, though, is that in order to offer even a modicum of security and so to perform any kind of healing or pain-soothing role, identity must belie its origin; it must deny being 'just a surrogate' – it needs to conjure up a phantom of the self-same community which it has come to replace. Identity sprouts on the graveyard of communities, but flourishes thanks to the promise of a resurrection of the dead.

A life dedicated to the search for identity is full of sound and fury. 'Identity' means standing out: being different, and through that difference unique – and so the search for identity cannot but divide and separate. And yet the vulnerability of individual identities and the precariousness of solitary identity-building prompt the identity-builders to seek pegs on which they can together hang their individually experienced fears and anxieties, and having done that, perform the exorcism rites in the company of other similarly afraid and anxious individuals. Whether such 'peg communities' provide what it is hoped they offer – collective insurance against individually confronted uncertainties – is a moot question; but no doubt marching shoulder to shoulder along a street or two, mounting a barricade in the company of others or rubbing elbows in crowded trenches may supply a momentary respite from loneliness. With good, bad, or no results, something at least has been done; one can derive some comfort from having refused to offer a sitting target and from having raised one's hands against the blows. Little wonder, therefore, that – as Jonathan Friedman warns us – in our fast globalizing world 'one thing that is not happening is that boundaries are disappearing. Rather, they seem to be erected on every new street corner of every declining neighbourhood of our world.'[6]

Despite the claims of the boundary guards, the bound-aries they protect have not been drawn to fence off and defend the distinctiveness of the already existing identities. As the great Norwegian anthropologist Frederick Barth explained, the opposite is the rule: the ostensibly shared 'communal' identities are after-effects or by-products of forever unfinished (and all the more feverish and ferocious for that reason) boundary drawing. It is only when the border poles are being dug in and the guns are aimed at trespassers that the myths of the borders' antiquity are spun and the recent cultural/political origins of identity are carefully covered up by the 'genesis stories'. This stratagem attempts to belie the fact that (to quote Stuart Hall)[7] one thing that the idea of identity does *not* signal is a 'stable core of the self, unfolding from the beginning to end through all the vicissitudes of history without change.'

Contemporary seekers of community are doomed to share Tantalus' lot; their purpose is bound to elude them, and it is their own earnest and zealous effort to grasp it that prompts it to recede. The hope of respite and tran-quillity which makes the community of their dreams so enticing will be dashed each time they declare, or are told, that the communal home they have sought has been found. The agonies of Tantalus will be joined, and made more agonizing yet, by those of Sisyphus. 'The really existing community' will be unlike their dreams – more like their opposite: it will add to their fears and insecurity instead of quashing them or putting them to rest. It will call for twenty-four hours a day vigilance and a daily resharpening of swords; for struggle, day in day out, to keep the aliens off the gates and to spy out and hunt down the turncoats in their own midst. And to add a final touch of irony, it is only through all that pugnacity, wolf-crying and sword-brandishing that the feeling of being *in* a community, of *being a community*, may be kept lingering and protected from evaporation. Homely cosiness is to be sought, day in day out, on the front line.

It is as if the sword thrust to the East of Eden still stood there, swirling ominously. By the sweat of your brow you may gain your daily bread – but no amount of sweating will ever reopen the closed gate to communal innocence, pristine sameness and tranquillity.

It is not as though we are likely to stop knocking at that gate and hoping to force it open. Not as long as we are as we presently are and as long as the world we inhabit is as it presently is.

Using Paul Klee's drawing as his inspiration, Walter Benjamin gave the following description of 'the Angel of History':

> his face is turned towards the past. Where we perceive a chain of events, he sees one single catastrophe which keeps piling up wreckage upon wreckage and hurls it in front of his feet. The angel would like to stay, awaken the dead, and make whole what has been smashed. But a storm is blowing from the Paradise; it has got hold of his wings with such violence that the angel can no longer close them. This storm irresistibly propels him into the future to which his back is turned, while the pile of debris before him grows skyward.[8]

The Angel of History moves with his back turned to the future, and so his eyes fixed to the past. He moves because since he left the paradise he cannot stop – he has not seen a sight agreeable enough to make him wish to pause and admire it at rest. What keeps him moving is disgust and repulsion for what he sees: the all-too-visible horrors of the past, not the lure of the future which he can neither clearly see nor fully appreciate. Progress, Benjamin implies, is not a chase after the birds in the sky, but a frantic urge to fly away from the corpses spattered over past battlefields.

If Walter Benjamin's reading of the meaning of 'progress' is correct, as I believe it is, then – as human happiness goes – history is neither a straight line nor a cumulative process, as its famed 'Whig version' wished us to believe. Repulsion, not attraction, being history's principal moving force, historical change happens because humans are mortified and annoyed by what they find painful and unpalatable in their condition, because they do not wish these conditions to persist, and because they seek the way to mollify or redress their suffering. Getting rid of what, momentarily, pains us most brings relief – but that respite is as a rule short-lived since the 'new and improved' condition quickly reveals its own, previously invisible and unanticipated, unpleasant aspects and brings new reasons to worry. In addition, one person's meat is another person's poison, and people in flight are hardly ever unanimous in their selection of which realities need attention and reform. Each step away from the present will be eyed with enthusiasm by some, with apprehension by others. 'Progress' is a prominent member of the family of 'hotly contested concepts'. The balance of the past, the assessment of the present and the appreciation of the futures are all conflict-ridden and strewn with ambivalence.

There is good reason to conceive of the course of history as pendulum-like, even if in other respects it may be portrayed as linear: freedom and security, both equally pressing and indispensable, happen to be hard to reconcile without friction – and considerable friction most of the time. These two qualities are, simultaneously, complementary and incompatible; the likelihood of their falling into conflict has always been and will forever be as high as the need for their reconciliation. Though many forms of human togetherness have been tried in the course of history, none has succeeded in finding a flawless solution to this truly 'squaring the circle' kind of task.

Promoting security always calls for the sacrifice of freedom, while freedom can only be expanded at the expense of security. But security without freedom equals slavery (and in addition, without an injection of freedom, proves to be in the end a highly insecure kind of security); while freedom without security equals being abandoned and lost (and in the end, without an injection of security, proves to be a highly unfree kind of freedom). This circumstance gives philosophers a headache with no known cure. It also makes living together conflict-ridden, as security sacrificed in the name of freedom tends to be *other people's* security; and freedom sacrificed in the name of security tends to be *other people's* freedom.

2

Rerooting the Uprooted

Pico della Mirandola put down in pen the text of a speech which neither God, the speaker, nor Adam, the spoken to, took care to record. It went, roughly, like this: 'The other creatures have a defined nature prescribed by me. You may determine your own limits according to your own will . . . Like a free and sovereign artificer, you can fashion your own form out of your own substance.' The message of that unrecorded speech was breathtakingly exhilarating news for the men of substance, though not at all exciting for all the rest, who did not have enough substance to 'fashion their own form' freely and 'according to their own will'. The year was 1486, the place was Italy sending its ships to the far corners of the world so that the shipowners, their courtiers and passengers (though not the sailors or the dockers) could get richer by the year and view the world as their oyster. Modern individuality of the ecclesiastical canon: the God of the Bible meant a sentence of untied and unfixed existence as retribution and punishment. The Renaissance God speaking through Pico portrayed that sentence as reward and an Act of Grace. If the biblical text was but a half-truth, its Renaissance correction was no better.

   In their study of the new era of inequalities, Jean-Paul Fitoussi and Pierre Rosanvallon ponder the 'ambivalence of modern individualism':

It is, at the same time, a vector of the emancipation of individuals, enhancing their autonomy and making them into the bearers of rights, and a factor of growing insecurity, making everybody accountable for the future and bound to give life a sense no longer being preshaped by anything outside.[9]

Fitoussi and Rosanvallon were not the first to note the Janus-like face of the individualization which was to become the trademark of (at least European) modernity, but they expressed the inner conflict it carried more sharply than most other writers. Like all other departures gathered under the rubric of the 'civilizing process', individualization was, as human values go, a trade-off. The goods exchanged in the course of individualization were security and freedom: freedom was on offer in exchange for security – though it did not necessarily look like that, not from the start and most certainly not for Pico della Mirandola and others looking and speaking from similarly elevated watch towers which the all-too-audible groans 'down there' on the ground could not reach. Given their new resourcefulness, and hence their distended self-confidence, freedom seemed to the high and mighty to be the best warrant of security imaginable; it went without saying that the foolproof recipe for *both* freedom and security was the cutting and shaking off of the few hands-tying bonds that remained. Freedom does not feel too risky as long as things go, obediently, the way one wishes them to go. Freedom is, after all, the ability to get things done according to one's wishes, with no one else able to resist the result, let alone to undo it.

The concubinate of freedom and security looks different, though, when watched from the direction of those many who find themselves sharing the plight of the Hebrew slaves in Egypt, told by the Pharaoh to go on producing bricks while being refused the straw needed to make them; men and women who find the rights they have been told to carry and enjoy pretty useless when it comes to making their ends meet. Individualization could be lavish and generously indiscriminate in thrusting the gift of personal liberty into every stretched hand – but the package deal of freedom *cum* security (or, more to the point, security *through* freedom) was not on general offer. It stayed available only to selected customers. The chance to enjoy freedom without paying the harsh and forbidding price of insecurity (or at least with no creditors demanding payment on the spot) was a privilege of the few; but these few set the tone of the emancipation idea for centuries to come. The tone began to change perceptibly only after a long period of genuine or putative 'bourgeoisification' of the proletariat had ground to a halt and then gone into reverse, while the gradual yet relentless process of the 'proletarianizing of the bourgeoisie', as Richard Rorty suggests, had taken off.

This does not mean that the privileged few who could enjoy both personal freedom and existential security (a luxury denied to the rest) had no reason for discontent. Sigmund Freud's long series of case studies can be read as *cahiers des doléances* of the rich and powerful who, having conquered the world outside, found its tough, stubborn and hard-to-shift garrisons inside their homes (and particularly inside their bedrooms) all the more spiteful and unendurable. *Das Unbehagen in der Kultur* (*Civilization and its Discontents*) summarizes their complaints: to enjoy the twin gifts of social freedom and personal safety, one must play the game of sociality according to such rules as deny free vent to lusts and passions. In the 'life politics' of Freud's patients (as Sigmund Freud would have said, had Anthony Giddens's terms been available at the time) the epic conflict of freedom and security surfaces above all as, perhaps solely as, sexual repression. Presenting the constraints socially imposed on sexual desire as the last rampart of unfreedom, Freud of *Das Unbehagen* expatiated on their unavoidability. Once singled out and named, they could however be easily recast as one more item in the 'unfinished project of modernity'. The ostensibly necessary defensive fortifications of civilized life have quickly turned into the next strategic target of the ongoing wars of emancipation; into another obstacle to be cleared out of the way of freedom's unstoppable progress.

Just a short time before he penned *Das Unbehagen* Freud sent to the printers another great synthesis: *Die Zukunft einer Illusion* (*The Future of an Illusion*). The two books together marked a great shift in Freud's interests. By his own admission, after a long psychotherapeutic detour, armed with the insights accumulated in the course of psychoanalytical practice, he returned to the cultural problems which had fascinated him long before. Unlike *Das Unbehagen*, which was a sustained attempt to articulate the collision between freedom and security as sedimented in the neuroses of psychotherapy patients, *Die Zukunft* cast its nets much wider. More correctly, it tried to develop a sustained argument for the unavoidability of social constraints on human freedom, based on the 'objective analysis' of the plight of all those who would never visit the psychoanalytical clinics. Freud had no clinical experience of the kinds of people who, in his argument, made constraints inescapable; but it was in the nature of the argument as developed in *Die Zukunft* that such experience was not called for. The focus of Freud's interest here was what Talcott Parsons would later call 'the functional prerequisites' of the system – and so Freud could, and did, leave the notes of psychoanalytical sessions aside and draw directly from the old and venerable post-

Hobbesian tradition of 'enlightened opinion' (more precisely, intellectual folklore) that was unanimous in its conviction that while some selected specimens of humankind could master the art of self-monitoring, all the rest, and that means the overwhelming majority, need coercion to stay alive and to let others live.

Die Zukunft[10] proceeds from the same assumption which a few months later was to serve as the starting point for *Das Unbehagen*: 'every civilization must be built up on coercion and renunciation of instinct.' Freud is careful however 'to distinguish between privations which affect everyone and privations which do not affect everyone but only groups, classes or even single individuals'. To the first category Freud assigns the kind of sufferings which he would later present more fully in *Das Unbehagen* – tribulations gleaned during psychoanalytical sessions with the selected Viennese clientele, but assumed nevertheless to have class-independent causes and thus to be shared universally by all. The bitterly, often violently resented privations of the second (non-universal, class-bound) kind derive from the fact that in a given culture 'the satisfaction of one portion of its participants depends upon the suppression of another, and perhaps larger, portion.' Without the privations of the first kind, civilization looked to Freud logically incoherent and so inconceivable. But he seemed to entertain no hope either for a civilization managing to do without recourse to the coercion of the second sort; this is because, in the opinion which Freud shared with the designers and the managers of the modern order,

> masses are lazy and unintelligent; they have no love for instinctual renunciation, and they are not to be convinced by argument of its inevitability; and the individuals composing them support one another in giving free rein to their indiscipline . . .

To put it briefly, there are two widespread human
characteristics which are responsible for the fact that the
regulations of civilization can only be maintained by a
certain degree of coercion – namely, that men are not
spontaneously fond of work and that arguments are of no
avail against their passions.

Indeed, as the French say – *deux poids, deux mesures*; in
the case of 'the masses', naturally lazy and deaf to the
voice of reason, refusal to give free rein to their natural
proclivities is an unambiguous blessing. As the 'masses'
go, the received wisdom of modern times rehearsed in *Die
Zukunft* would not contemplate any renegotiation of the
portion of allowed freedom. Mass rebellion is not at all
like individual neuroses suffered in solitude by the sexually
repressed clients of psychoanalytical clinics. It is not a
matter for psychotherapy, but for law and order; not a
task for psychoanalysts, but for policemen.

The modern – capitalist – arrangement of human
cohabitation was Janus-faced; one face was emancipatory,
the other coercive, each being turned towards a different
section of society. For the companions of Pico della
Mirandola, civilization was the clarion call to 'make oneself what one wishes', and drawing limits to that freedom
of self-assertion was perhaps an unavoidable but regrettable obligation of the civilized order, a price worth paying. To the 'lazy and passion-ridden masses' civilization
meant, first and foremost, a curbing of the morbid predi-
lections which they were assumed to harbour and which,
if unloosed, would explode orderly cohabitation. To the
two sections of modern society, the self-assertion offered
and the discipline demanded were mixed in sharply differing proportions.

To put it bluntly: the emancipation of some called for
the suppression of others. And this is exactly what hap-

pened: this happening went down in history under some-what euphemistic name of the 'industrial revolution'. The 'masses' were wrested out of the stiff old routine (the habit-ruled web of communal interactions) to be squeezed into a stiff new routine (of the task-ruled factory floor), where their suppression could better serve the cause of the suppressors' emancipation. Old routines were no good for the purpose – they were much too autonomous, governed by their own tacit and non-negotiable logic, and much too resistant to manipulation and change since too many strings of human interaction were intertwined in every act so that to pull one many others had to be shifted or broken. The question was not so much how to make the work-shy keen to work (no one had to teach the future factory hands that life meant a sentence of hard labour), but how to make them ready to labour in a brand new and unfamiliar repressive setting.

In order to fit new clothes, the would-be labourers had first to be made into a 'mass': stripped naked of the old dress of communally supported habits. The war declared on community was waged in the name of freeing the individual from the inertia of the mass. But the genuine even if unspoken end of that war was very much the opposite of the declared goal: to take apart the pattern- and role-setting powers of community so that the human units stripped of their individuality could be condensed into the labouring mass. The inborn 'laziness' of the 'masses' was but a (feeble) excuse. As I argued in *Work, Consumerism and New Poor* (1998), the 'work ethic' of the early industrial era was a desperate attempt to reconstitute in the cold and impersonal setting of the factory, through command, surveillance and punitive regime, the self-same workmanship which in the dense network of communal intercourse came to the craftsmen, artisans and tradesmen matter-of-factly.

The nineteenth century, the century of great disloca-
tions, disencumbering, disembeddedness and uprooting
(as well as of desperate attempts to re-encumber, re-
embed and re-root) was nearing its end when Thorstein
Veblen[11] spoke up on behalf of the apparently extinct
'instinct of workmanship' which 'is present in all men'
and 'asserts itself under very adverse circumstances', in
order to seek repair of the harm done. 'Instinct of workmanship' was a name Veblen chose for a natural 'taste for
effective work, and a distaste for futile effort', in his view
common to all humans. Far from being naturally lazy and
work-shy, as Freud insisted in unison with a long string of
modern fault-finders and grumblers, people had, well
before all the reprobation and preaching started,

> a sense of the merit of serviceability or efficiency and of the
> demerit of futility, waste or incapacity . . . [T]he instinct of
> workmanship expresses itself not so much in insistence on
> substantial usefulness as in an abiding sense of the odious-
> ness and aesthetic impossibility of what is obviously futile.

If we all take pride in work well done, we all also have,
so Veblen suggests, an inborn repulsion to purposeless
drudgery, futile effort, meaningless bustle. This was also
true of the 'masses', accused since the advent of modern
(capitalist) industry of the mortal sin of sloth. If Veblen is
right and reluctance to work violates human instincts,
then something must have been done, and done resolutely
and forcefully, for the 'really existing' conduct of the
'masses' to give credibility to the charge of idleness. That
'something' was the slow yet relentless dismantling/falling
apart of the community, that tangled web of human
interactions which endowed work with meaning, forging
mere *exertion* into a meaningful *work, into an action with
purpose*, that web which made the difference, as Veblen

would say, between 'exploits' (linked to the 'concepts of dignity, worth or honour') and 'drudgery' (linked to none of such things and thereby felt as futile).

According to Max Weber, the constitutive act of modern capitalism was the separation of business from the household – which meant, simultaneously, the separation of producers from the sources of their livelihood (as Karl Polanyi added, invoking Karl Marx's insight). That double act set the actions of profit-making, as well as making one's livelihood, free from the web of moral and emotional, family and neighbourly bonds – but by the same token it also emptied such actions of all the meanings it used to carry before. What used to be an 'exploit' in Veblen's terms turned into 'drudgery'. It was no longer clear to the craftsmen and artisans of yesterday what 'work well done' would mean, and there was no longer 'dignity, worth or honour' attached to 'doing it well'. Following the soulless routine of the factory floor, watched by no kinsman or neighbour but solely by the constantly suspicious and rat-smelling foreman, going through machine-dictated motions with no chance to admire the product of one's exertion, let alone to sit in judgement on its quality, rendered the effort all but 'futile'; and a futile effort was what the instinct of workmanship prompted humans to abhor and resent at all times. It was at that all-too-human dislike of futility and meaninglessness that the charge of laziness, raised against men, women and children torn away from their home environment and subjected to a rhythm they neither set nor understood, was in fact targeted. The reputed 'nature' of factory hands stood accused for the effects of the unnaturalness of the new social setting. What the managers of capitalist industry and the moral preachers who rushed to their help wished to achieve through the 'work ethics' they set up and preached was to force or inspire factory hands to perform

'futile chores' with the same dedication and self-abandon-
ment with which they used to pursue their 'work well
done'.

For the entrepreneur, the separation of business from
the household was a genuine emancipation. His hands
had been unbound, the sky was the sole limit beyond
which his ambition did not dare to reach. In pursuing
what reason told him was the road to greater wealth, the
exuberant and self-confident 'someone who makes things
happen' would no longer have to reckon with received
notions of communal duty, now dismissed as outmoded
tradition (if not as ignorant superstition). The separation
of livelihood from the household, the other face of the
first separation, was not however intended as, nor did it
feel like, an emancipation: as an untying of the hands and
a setting free of the individual. It was meant to be, and it
felt like, an act of dispossession, an uprooting and eviction
from a defensible home. Men and women had first to be
cut away from the web of communal bonds which
cramped their moves, so that they could be redeployed as
factory crews later. But redeployment was their destination, and the freedom of undetermination was but a
brief transitory stage between two equally stiff steel
casings.

Modern capitalism, as Marx and Engels memorably put
it, 'melted all solids'; self-sustained and self-reproducing
communities were high on the list of solids lined up for
liquefaction. But the melting job was not an end in itself:
solids were liquefied so that new solids, more solid than
the melted ones, could be cast. If for the selected few the
advent of the modern order meant the opening of a
breathtakingly vast expanse for individual self-assertion –
for the great majority it augured reallocation from one stiff
and narrow setting into another. Once the communal ties
holding them in place had been torn away, that majority

was to be subjected to an altogether different routine, blatantly contrived, supported by naked coercion and carrying little sense in terms of 'dignity, worth or honour'.

It was, to say the least, naive to expect the disinherited to embrace the contrived and imposed routine with the same placidity with which they used to follow the rhythms of communal life. A stern and closely supervised disciplining regime had to fill the void which had opened where once consent and 'natural understanding' had ruled the course of human life. This is how John Stuart Mill[12] summed up the prevailing mood of the time (which he deeply resented):

> The lot of the poor, in all things which affect them collectively, should be regulated for them, not by them . . . It is the duty of the higher classes to think for them, and to take responsibility of their lot . . . [in order that] they may resign themselves . . . to a truthful *insouciance*, and repose under the shadow of their protectors . . . The rich should be *in loco parentis* to the poor, guiding and restraining them like children.

More than a century later, looking back at the early decades of the brave new world of capitalist modernity, historian John Foster[13] captured the essence of the great transformation when pointing out that

> The overriding priority was to bind the emergent labour force to the new employer class – and to do so during a period in which the old self-imposed disciplines of peasant–craft society were (at one and the same time) both disintegrating and still dangerously potent.

Watching with irony and scepticism the frenzy with which reformers and revolutionaries dismantled the extant social arrangements, Alexis de Tocqueville suggested that

while declaring a war of attrition against the 'backwaters'
and 'parochiality' of the peasant–craft society, the rising
entrepreneurial class was kicking a dead horse; indeed,
local community had been in an advanced state of putre-
faction well before the building of the new order took off
in earnest. That might have been the case, and yet whatever the state of its disintegration, the local community
went on being felt to be 'dangerously potent' throughout
the long years that it took to drill yesterday's peasants–
craftsmen into the new factory discipline. That feeling
beefed up the fervour and ingenuity with which the owners and managers of industry fought to regulate the conduct of their labour force and to stifle all manifestations
of spontaneity and free will.

It has been said, as John Stuart Mill opined, the 'higher classes'
put themselves *in loco parentis* of the poor and the indolent,
who, as they believed, could not be trusted with the
precious (and so threatened if put in the wrong hands)
toy of freedom. The duty of parents is to guide and
restrain, but in order to take that duty seriously and
perform it responsibly they must first of all surveille and
supervise.

It has been said of children that, like fish, they should
be seen and not heard. And so through most of its history
modernity did its job under the auspices of 'panoptical'
power, exacting discipline by continuous surveillance. The
essential principle of the panopticon is the inmates' belief
that they are permanently under observation and that no
departure from the routine, however minuscule and triv-
ial, will pass unnoticed. For that belief to be kept alive the
surveillants had to spend most of their time at their
observation posts, just as parents cannot leave home for
long without fear of children's mischief. The panoptical
model of power tied the subordinates to the spot, the
place where they could be watched and instantly punished

for any breach of routine. But it also tied their surveillants to the spot, the place from which they had to do their watching and apportion punishment.

The era of great transformation was, to put it in a nutshell, an era of *engagement*. The ruled were dependent on the rulers, but the rulers no less depended on the ruled. For better or worse, the two sides were tied to each other and neither could easily opt out of the wedlock – however cumbersome and repulsive it might feel. Divorce was not a realistic option for either side. When in a flash of inspiration Henry Ford made his historic decision to double his workers' wages, what he was after was a double bind which would tie them to *his* factories more strongly and more securely than the mere need of livelihood, which could be met by other employers as well. Ford's power and wealth were no more extensive and no more solid than his immense factories, heavy machines and massive labour force; he could not afford to lose either. It took some time before both sides, by many trials and more errors still, learned that truth. But once the truth had been learned, the inconvenience and the high and rising cost of panoptical power (and, more generally, of domination-through-engagement) became apparent.

A marriage where both sides know that it has been tied together for a long time to come, and neither of the partners is free to take it apart, is by necessity a site of perpetual conflict. The chances that the partners will be of the same mind on all matters that may arise in the unforeseeable future are as small as the probability that one of the partners will in all matters give way to the will of the other, making no attempt to win a better deal. And so there will be numerous confrontations, head-on battles and guerrilla sallies. Only in extreme cases, though, are the war actions likely to lead to the ultimate attrition of one or both partners: an awareness that such attrition can happen and the wish that it preferably should not will in all probability be enough to cut the 'schismogenetic chain' just before the ultimate happens ('since we are bound to stay together whatever happens, let's rather try to make our togetherness liveable'). So alongside the internecine war there will also be long periods of truce, and between them bouts of bargaining and negotiation. And there will be renewed attempts to compromise on a shared set of rules acceptable to all.

Two tendencies accompanied modern capitalism through the whole of its history, though their relative strength and prominence varied over time. One tendency has been already signalled: a consistent effort to replace the 'natural understanding' of bygone community, the nature-regulated rhythm of farming and the tradition-regulated routine of the craftsman's life by an artificially designed and coercively imposed and monitored routine. The second tendency was a much less consistent (and belatedly undertaken) attempt to resuscitate or create *ab nihilo* a 'community feeling', this time within the framework of the new power structure.

The first tendency culminated by the beginning of the twentieth century in the assembly line and Frederick Taylor's 'time and motion study' and 'scientific organization of work', which was aimed at decoupling productive performance from the motives and sentiments of the performers. Producers were to be exposed to the impersonal rhythm of the machine, which would set the pace of movement and determine every motion; no room was to be left, or would need to be reserved, for personal discretion and choice. The role of initiative, dedication and cooperation, even of the 'live skills' of the operators (better transferred to the machine), was to be reduced to the minimum. The streamlining and routinizing of the production process, the impersonality of the worker-machine relation, the elimination of all dimensions of the productive role except the set production tasks, and the resulting homogeneity of labourers' actions combined into the very opposite of the communal setting in which pre-industrial labour was inscribed. The factory floor was to be the machine-run equivalent of bureaucracy, which according to the ideal model sketched by Max Weber aimed at a total irrelevancy of the social bonds and commitments entered into and entertained outside the office building and office hours. The results of work were not to be affected by factors as flickery and unreliable as the 'instinct of workmanship' with its hunger for honour, worth and dignity, and, above all, its aversion to futility.

The second tendency ran parallel to the first, starting early in the 'model villages' of a few philanthropists who associated industrial success with a 'feeling good' factor among the labourers. Instead of relying solely on the grinding coercive powers of the machine, they put a wager on the moral standards of labourers, their religious piety, the ampleness of their family lives and their trust in the boss-patron. Model villages built around factories were equipped with decent dwellings, but also with chapels, primary schools, hospitals and basic social amenities – all predesigned by the factory owners along with the rest of the production complex. The bid was to recreate community centred around the place of work and, conversely, to make factory employment into a 'whole life' pursuit.

Philanthropists, viewed by their contemporaries as 'utopian socialists' and for that reason applauded by some as pioneers of moral reform, viewed by others with suspicion and ostracized for subversion, hoped to blunt the depersonalizing and dehumanizing edge of the advancing machine age and preserve something of the old paternal, benign and benevolent master–apprentice relationship and community spirit in the harsh climate of competition and profit-making. Ethically motivated philanthropists remained marginal to the main thrust of capitalist development. It soon became apparent that they were swimming against the tide: the death sentence passed on community was irrevocable, while the odds against its rising from the dead were overwhelming. It took a century or so for the second tendency to surface once more, this time as an effort to salvage the flagging efficiency of factory work in the victorious and no longer contested capitalist industry, rather than, as a century earlier, to arrest the bulldozing of the communal tradition by an advancing capitalist order.

In the 1930s, the 'human relations school' was founded in industrial sociology, following Elton Mayo's experiments at Hawthorne Enterprises. Mayo's discovery was that none of the physical aspects of the working environment, not even the material incentives given the most prominent place in Frederick Taylor's strategy, influenced the rise in productivity and eliminated conflicts as much as spiritual factors: a friendly and 'homely' atmosphere in the workplace, attention paid by managers and foremen to the shifting moods of the workers and care taken to explain to the employees the significance of their contributions to the overall productive effects. One may say that the forgotten and neglected importance of community for meaningful action, and of the 'instinct of workmanship' for good work, were thereby rediscovered as as-yet-untapped resources in the perpetual effort to improve the cost-and-effect relationship.

What secured an almost overnight success for Mayo's proposals was his suggestion that bonuses and wage increases, as well as the pernickety (and costly) minute-by-minute supervision, wouldn't be that important after all – so long as the employers managed to evoke that 'we are all in the same boat' feeling among employees, to promote loyalty to the company and impress them with the significance of individual performance for the joint effort; in short, if they respected the workers' craving for dignity, worth and honour and their innate resentment of futile and meaningless routine. The good news was that job satisfaction and a friendly atmosphere might go further than strict rule enforcement and ubiquitous surveillance in promoting efficiency at work and in staving off the threat of recurrent industrial conflict, while making more 'economic sense' in purely actuarial terms than the drill methods they replaced.

The famed 'Fordist factory' attempted to synthesize both tendencies, and so to combine the best of both worlds, sacrificing as little as possible of the potential of either 'scientific organization' or communal-style togetherness. In Tönnies' terms, it aimed at reforging *Kürwille* into *Wesenwille*, at 'naturalizing' the blatantly artificial, abstractly designed rational patterns of conduct. For about half a century, and particularly through the 'glorious three decades' of the 'social compact' which accompanied postwar reconstruction, the 'Fordist factory' served as a model, of the ideal pursued with varying success by all other capitalist enterprises.

The two tendencies, one strictly and explicitly anti-communal and the other flirting and dabbling with the idea of community's new avatar, stood for two alternative forms of management. But the assumption that social processes in general, and productive work in particular, needed to be *managed* rather than left to their own momentum was not in question. Neither was the belief that the duty of 'guiding and restraining' was an obligatory ingredient of the employers' position *in loco parentis*. For the greater part of its history, modernity was an era of 'social engineering' in which the spontaneous emergence and reproduction of order was not to be trusted; with the self-regenerating institutions of premodern society all but gone forever, the sole conceivable order was an order designed using the power of reason and maintained by day-to-day monitoring and management.

3

Times of Disengagement, or the Great Transformation Mark Two

Since the beginning of modern times, management has been not a matter of choice, but a necessity. But, as Karl Marx observed, there is no need for the conductor of a symphony orchestra to own the violins and the trumpets. One could easily turn this observation around and point out that neither is there a need for the owners of orchestral instruments to take upon themselves the complex tasks of conducting. As it happens, very few conductors have been known to try to buy out the instruments of their orchestras; but the owners of orchestras and concert halls have been eager as a rule to hire their conductors rather than doing the job themselves. As soon as they could afford it, capitalist entrepreneurs shifted managerial chores to hired servants.

Just before the beginning of World War Two, James Burnham gave articulate expression to what was already common knowledge, when he proclaimed that the 'managerial revolution' had already happened, and was about to end in the managers' victory. Profits, Burnham suggested, might still be flowing as before into the owners' pockets, but the day-to-day running of affairs had become the prerogative of the managers, and no one would any longer dare or wish to interfere. Some managers might own shares in the companies they ran, some might be, legally

speaking, employees pure and simple, but for the allocation of power that was irrelevant. Power consists in
decision-making and resides with those who make the
decisions. And so power belonged to the managers.

After more than half a century, Burnham's *Managerial
Revolution* reads as the summation of the long experience
of modern power struggles and of the strategies deployed
in their course. The substance of modern power did not
lie in legal titles to ownership, and modern power struggles did not consist of the scramble for more possessions.
Modern power was first and foremost about the entitlement to manage people, to command, to set the rules of
conduct and extort obedience to the rules. The original
personal union between ownership and management was
a matter of historical coincidence, and later developments
showed it to be such. That initial union beclouded rather
than revealed the truth of modern power. Obliquely,
Burnham paid homage to the passion for order building
and order servicing as the driving force of modern society;
and to the direct engagement with people, to the activity
of patterning, surveilling, monitoring and directing their
actions as the paramount method of order design, building
and maintenance. He did so by replacing the model of
capitalist modernity driven by profit-making motives with
that of *modern* capitalism driven by the urge to substitute
a contrived/designed routine for the communally sustained tradition.

It so happens that social forms are the most visible (and
so the most likely to be noted and recognized for what they
were all along) when they emerge from the carapace inside
which they gestated; when they reach maturity and come
into their own. The moment of maturation, though, is
more often than not the beginning of decline and demise.
The story of the 'great engagement', of the modern social-
engineering/managerial adventure, was no exception.

A few decades passed, lived in the shadow of war destruction and postwar reconstruction, and it became clear that the turn of managers had arrived to shed the awkward and cumbersome managerial duties previously dropped on their shoulders by capital's titular owners. The managers set out in earnest to repeat the capital owners' vanishing act. After the era of 'great engagement', the times of 'great disengagement' have arrived. The times of high speed and acceleration, shrinking terms of commitment, of 'flexibility', 'downsizing' and 'outsourcing'. The times of staying together only 'until further notice' and as long (never longer) 'as the satisfaction lasts'.

'Deregulation' is the talk of the town and the strategic principle praised and actively deployed by everyone in power. 'Deregulation' is in demand because the powerful do not want to be 'regulated' – have their freedom of choice limited and freedom of movement constrained; but also (perhaps in the first place) because they are *no longer interested in regulating others*. Policing order and servicing it have become a hot potato which is gladly disposed of by those who are strong enough to get rid of the cumbersome ballast and promptly thrust it into the hands of those lower down the hierarchy who are too weak to refuse the poisonous gift.

These days, domination does not rest primarily on engagement-and-commitment; on the capacity of rulers to watch closely the movements of the ruled and to coerce them into obedience. It has acquired a new, much less troublesome and less costly – since requiring little servicing – foundation: in the uncertainty of the ruled as to what move, if any, their rulers may make next. As Pierre Bourdieu has repeatedly pointed out, the state of permanent *precarité* – insecurity of social standing, uncertainty about the future of one's livelihood and the overwhelming feeling of 'no grip on the present' – combine into an incapacity to make plans and to act on them. When the threat of unilateral change of the rules or a termination of the current arrangements by those who decide the setting in which life tasks need to be pursued hangs perpetually over the heads of those who pursue them, the chances of resistance to the moves of power-holders, and particularly of steady, organized and solidary resistance, are minimal – virtually non-existent. The power-holders have nothing to fear and so feel little need for the costly and unwieldy, panopticon-style 'factories of obedience'. Amidst uncertainty and insecurity, discipline (or, rather, submission to the 'there is no alternative' condition) is self-propelling and self-reproducing and needs no foremen or corporals to supervise its constantly replenished supplies.

The dismantling of panopticons augurs a great leap forward on the road to the greater freedom of the individual. It is experienced, however, to say the least, as a mixed blessing, or a blessing too thoroughly disguised for enjoyment.

The panoptical regime, well-nigh universal during the 'great engagement' era, was cruel and demeaning: it made even perfectly rational productive exertions feel like 'futile drudgery' and stripped work of its 'honour, worth and dignity' bestowing capacity. It had, though, certain advantages for the victims – it brought them benefits which were hardly noticed at the time and have only recently become salient through their disappearance.

Its anticipated permanence made the mutual engagement into a trustworthy frame in which those on the receiving end of the panoptical arrangement could also confidently inscribe their hopes and dreams of a better future; the solidity of mutual engagement made the struggle for better terms worthwhile. Since each of the sides was similarly 'tied to the place' and unfree to move,

it made good sense for both to seek an acceptable accom-
modation rather than risk confrontation and war (even in
Auschwitz, where the sinister potential of the panopticon
revealed all its horrifying malignancy, the inmates who –
unlike their Jewish and Gypsy co-prisoners – expected to
stay in the camp and work for the long time to come
rather than be sent to their death at any moment managed
to win improvements in their conditions through solidary
resistance). No doubt the routine enforced by the 'factories of discipline' was intensely disliked and resented. But,
as Richard Sennett reminds us,

> intense negotiations over these schedules preoccupied both
> the United Auto Workers Union and the management of
> General Motors . . . Routinized time had become an arena
> in which workers could assert their own demands, an arena
> of empowerment . . . Routine can demean, but it can also
> protect; routine can decompose labour, but it can also
> compose a life.[14]

Under new conditions, with the powers-that-be no
longer interested in the supervision and monitoring of the
routine and preferring to rely instead on the subordinates'
endemic lack of self-confidence, the constraints cramping
the subordinates' freedom have not become noticeably
looser; 'domination from the top', as Sennett points out,
has become 'shapeless' without losing any of its strength.[15]
As if to add insult to injury, the pain-inflicting forces keep
their grip as tight, perhaps tighter than before, but in
addition have also become invisible and virtually impossible to pinpoint, and so to confront and to fight them
back. The desperate struggle to mitigate the pain has to
be conducted in the dark and tends to be unfocused,
drifting from one accidental target to another, each
attempt without exception going wide of the mark, with

little real improvement promised even if it hits. The forces truly responsible for the pain can rest assured that however furious the responses provoked by the suffering they've caused, they will be deflected to other objects and hardly detract from their own freedom to act.

Half a century ago, students of the social sciences were introduced to the workings of the human psyche through serial experiments by behaviourist psychologists; hungry rats were sent through twisted corridors of a maze seeking a pellet of food placed each time in the same compartment of the labyrinth, so that the time they took to learn the right way (always the same single right way among many erroneous tracks) could be duly plotted. Only a few people objected then to the behaviourists' suggestion that what was true of the rats was equally true for humans, and the objections were few and far between not because the implied rat–human similarity was evident or universally believed, but because the behaviourists' laboratory setting was so strikingly similar to the human predicament as visualized at the time: solid, tough, impenetrable and immovable walls of a labyrinth with only a few passageways correct and many others leading astray; immutable rules determining a one-and-for-all location of the reward waiting at the far end of the chase; learning (memorizing and habitualizing) the skills of telling the right turns apart from the wrong ones being the essence of the art of life. The contrived plight of the rats-in-a-maze seemed a faithful laboratory replica of the daily predicament of humans-in-the-world. If today the behaviourist parallels have lost most of their persuasive power and are all but forgotten, it is not because the insinuations of spiritual kinship with rats have been belatedly found offensive for the human side of the comparison, but because the vision of a solid, cut-in-hard-rock labyrinth no longer chimes well with the experience ordinary humans have of the world in which

they live. A radically different metaphor, Edmund Jabès'
image of a desert in which the roads (many and criss-
crossing, and none of them signposted) are nothing but
thin files of the wanderers' footprints, liable to be swept
away by the desert winds, seems to fit that experience
much better.

In the world we inhabit at the threshold of the twenty-
first century, walls are far from solid and most certainly
not fixed once and for all; eminently mobile, they remind
the traveller-through-life of cardboard partitions or
screens meant to be repositioned over and over again
following successive changes in needs or whims. Alterna-
tively, one may say that there are cotton-wool skeins where
once steel casings stood fast in Max Weber's time; blows
will get through and the breach momentarily produced
will seal up a moment later. One may also think of a world
which has turned from being a rigorously impartial umpire
into one of the players, and one who, like all the rest of
the players fond of tricks, keeps his hand secret and is
keen to cheat if given a chance.

By far the toughest of the steely casings in which average life used to be inscribed was the social frame in which
one's livelihood was gained: the office or industrial plant,
the jobs done there, the skills needed to do them and the
daily routine of doing them. Solidly encased in that
frame, work could be reasonably seen as a vocation or a
life's mission: as the axis around which all the rest of life
rotated and along which all life pursuits were plotted. By
now this axis has been irreparably broken. Rather than
becoming 'flexible', as the spokespeople for the brave
new world would wish its new condition to be perceived,
it has turned fragile and friable. Nothing could (and
nothing should) be fixed to that axis with confidence –
trusting its durability would be naive and might prove
fatal. Even the most venerable offices and plants proud

their long and glorious past tend to vanish overnight and without notice; allegedly permanent and indispensable, 'cannot do without' jobs evaporate long before the work has been finished; skills once feverishly sought for, being in hot demand, age and are found unsellable well before their anticipated 'sell-by' date has expired; and job routines are turned upside down before they have been learned. The 'pellet of food' at the imagined end of the road moves or gets foul faster than even the most intelligent among the hungry rats manage to learn the paths leading to it . . .

The social frame of work and livelihood is not the only one that is falling apart, though. Everything else around seems to be in a whirlwind. To quote Sennett once more,[16] the place where the whole of life is conducted or hoped to be conducted 'springs into life with the wave of a developer's wand, flourishes, and begins to decay all within a generation.' In such a place (and more and more people come to know such places and their bitter atmosphere the hard way) no one 'becomes a long-term witness to another person's life'. The place may be physically crowded, and yet frighten and repel the residents by its moral emptiness. It is not just that the places appear from nowhere, on a site uninhabited in human memory, and that before the mortgage loan has been fully repaid they begin to decay, turning from the hospitable into the repellent and prompting the hapless residents into another bout of house-hunting. It is rather that nothing in the place stays the same for long, and nothing endures long enough to be fully taken in, to become familiar and to turn into the cosy, secure and comfortable envelope the community-hungry and home-thirsty selves have sought and hoped for. Gone are the friendly corner grocery shops; if they have managed to withstand the supermarket competition, their owners, managers, the faces behind the counter change much too often for any of them to harbour the permanence no longer to be found in the street. Gone are the friendly local bank or building society branches, replaced by anonymous and impersonal (ever more often electronically synthesized) voices on the other end of the telephone cable or 'user friendly', yet infinitely remote, nameless and faceless website icons. Gone is the friendly postman, knocking on the door six days a week and addressing the inhabitants by their names. In are the department stores and high-street chain shops, expected to survive from one friendly merger or hostile takeover to another, but in the meantime changing their staff at a pace which reduces to zero the chances of meeting the same salesperson twice.

It is not as though inside the family home things look more solid than in the street. As Yvonne Roberts acidly remarked, 'embarking on matrimony in the twenty-first century appears to be as wise as taking to the sea on a raft made of blotting paper' (*Observer*, 13 Feb. 2000). The chances that the family will survive any of its members gets slimmer by the year: the life-expectation of the individual mortal body seems an eternity by comparison. An average child has several sets of grandparents and several 'family homes' to choose between – each for 'time renting', like holiday apartments in fashionable seaside resorts. None of these feels like the true, 'one and only' home.

To sum up: gone are most of the steady and solidly dug-in orientation points which suggested a social setting that was more durable, more secure and more reliable than the timespan of an individual life. Gone is the certainty that 'we will meet again', that we will be meeting repeatedly and for a very long time to come – and that therefore society can be presumed to have a long memory and what we do to each other today will come to comfort us or grieve us in the future; that what we do to each other has more than episodic significance, since the consequences of our actions will stay with us long after the actions have apparently ended – surviving in the minds and deeds of witnesses who are not going to vanish.

All these and similar assumptions formed, so to speak, the 'epistemological foundation' of the experience of *community*; one would be tempted to say 'of a *closely knit community*', if this often used phrase were not pleonastic – no aggregate of human beings is experienced as 'community' unless it is 'closely knit' out of biographies shared through a long history and an even longer life expectation of frequent and intense interaction. It is such experience which is nowadays missing, and it is its absence that is reported as 'decline', 'demise' or 'eclipse' of community – as already noted by Maurice R. Stein in 1960: 'community ties become increasingly dispensable . . . [P]ersonal loyalties decrease their range with the successive weakening of national ties, regional ties, community ties, neighbourhood ties, family ties and finally, ties to a coherent image of one's self.'[17]

The kind of uncertainty, of dark premonitions and fears of the future that haunt men and women in the fluid, perpetually changing social environment in which the rules of the game change in the middle of the game without warning or legible pattern, does not unite the sufferers: it splits them and sets them apart. The pains it causes to the individuals do not add up, do not accumulate or condense into a kind of 'common cause' which could be pursued more effectively by joining forces and acting in unison. The decline of community is in this sense self-perpetuating; once it takes off, there are fewer and fewer stimuli to stem the disintegration of human bonds and seek ways to tie again what has been torn apart. The plight of individuals fighting it all alone may be painful and unprepossessing, but firm and binding commitments to act together seem to augur more harm than gain. The rafts may be discovered to be made of blotting paper when the chance of salvation has already been missed.

4

Secession of the Successful

The phrase above comes from Robert Reich's *The Work of Nations*: it refers to the new detachment, indifference, disengagement and indeed mental and moral exterritoriality of those who do not mind being left alone providing that the others, who think differently, don't bid for them to care and above all for a share in the perks of their 'do it yourself' life. Richard Rorty[18] suggests that having capitalized individually on their parents' collective and solidary battles, children of the generation who made it through the Great Depression settled in affluent suburbia and 'decided to pull up the drawbridge behind them'. Indeed, the children of the militants won their individual promotions thanks to the communal insurance against individual misfortune which their parents had put in place. They do not like to be reminded, though, how it happened that they came to be self-reliant; they see no reason why others should not become like them so long as they behave like they themselves do now. They reforge their own disgust of 'dependency' which they no longer need into a universal moral condemnation of dependency which the less fortunate need like the air they breathe and cannot do without. And so, as Rorty says,

> Under Presidents Carter and Clinton the Democratic Party has survived by distancing itself from the unions and from

any mention of redistribution, and moving into a sterile vacuum called 'the centre' . . . It is as if the distribution of income and wealth had become too scary a topic for any American politician . . . ever to mention . . . So the choice between the two major parties has come down to a choice between cynical lies and terrified silence.

Something happened which never occurred as a possibility to Menenius Agrippa when he harangued the plebeians to stay in Rome and abandon their plans to secede and leave the patricians on their own. Menenius Agrippa would be astonished to learn that in the end it was not the plebeians but the contemporary equivalents of the patricians of ancient Rome who (by design or by default, but never looking back since) decided to 'secede', to opt out from their commitments and wash their hands of their responsibilities. The present-day patricians no longer need the services of the community; indeed, they cannot see what staying *in and with* the community could offer which they have not already secured for themselves or still hope to secure through their own exploits, while they can think of quite a lot of assets which they might lose if they were to abide by the demands of communal solidarity.

Dick Pountain and David Robins[19] pick up the 'cool' mode as the symptom of mind and character of the 'secession of the successful'. When the 'cool' gained sudden popularity and spread like a bush-fire among the children of the post-Depression affluents, it bore the mask of a rebellion and moral renewal: it was a symbol of a militant detachment from a stale establishment content with where its past had brought it to and fast running out of new ideas. By now, however, the 'cool' has become the *Weltanschauung* of the mainstream, thoroughly conservative in its actions and the preferences which its actions exemplify, if not in its outspoken (and deceitful) self-praise. That increasingly conservative mainstream is backed by the awesome powers of the consumer market and whatever remains of the once autonomous political institutions. The 'cool', Pountain and Robins suggest, 'appears to be usurping the work ethic to install itself as the dominant mindset of advanced consumer capitalism'. 'Cool' means 'flight from feeling', 'from the messiness of real intimacy, into the world of the easy lay, the casual divorce, and non-possessive relationships'.

> Given a complete loss of faith in radical political alterna- tives, cool is now primarily about consumption. This is the missing 'cement' that fills the gaping contradiction – cool is the way to live with the lowered expectations by going shopping . . . Personal taste is elevated into a complete ethos; you are what you like, and what you therefore buy.

Though it carries many a trapping of personal auton- omy and is conducted under the 'I need more space' slogan, the flight from the 'messiness of real intimacy' is more akin to a herd-like stampede than to an individually conceived and undertaken journey of self-exploration. The secession is hardly ever lonely – the escapees are keen to join company with other escapees like them, and the standards of the escapee life tend to be as stiff and demanding as those which have been found oppressive in the life left behind; the facility of casual divorce spawns imperatives as inflexible and intractable (and potentially as displeasing) as the wedlock without the escape clause. The sole attraction of the self-chosen exile is the absence of commitments, and particularly long-term commitments of the kind that cramp freedom of movement in a com- munity with its 'messy intimacy'. With commitments replaced by fleeting encounters, the 'until further notice' or 'one night' (or one-day) stands, one can delete from calculation the effects which one's action might have on the lives of others. The future may be as hazy and impenetrable as before, but at least this otherwise discomforting trait does not matter much in a life lived as a string of episodes and a series of new beginnings.

Søren Kierkegaard[20] would probably find a striking affinity between the kind of life that lures the successful into secession, and the type of pathology he gleaned in the character of Don Giovanni as portrayed in the libretto of Mozart's opera. Don Juan's pleasure, as Kierkegaard saw it, was not the *possession* of women, but their *seduction*; Don Giovanni had no interest in the women already conquered – his pleasure stopped at the moment of triumph. Don Juan's sexual appetites were not necessarily more voracious or more insatiable than those of the next man; the point is, though, that the question of how great these appetites were was totally irrelevant to Don Juan's life formula, since his life was about keeping desire alive rather than about its satisfaction.

> Only in this manner can Don Juan become epic, in that he constantly finishes, and constantly begins again from the beginning, for his life is the sum of repellent moments which have no coherence, his life as moment is the sum of the moments, as the sum of the moments is the moment . . .

Choosing the seduction of women as a major pastime was, to be sure, but an accidental attribute of Don Juan's life plan; it could be easily replaced by altogether different kinds of pleasure without detracting a wit from Don Juna's life strategy. To constantly finish, and to begin again from the beginning – that was the essence of Don Giovanni's life formula, and to be consistently applied that formula required, more than anything else, that no attachments should be fixed and no commitments entered, that no consent should be given to bear the consequences of one's past pleasures: in other words, it postulated the *absence of community*. Don Juan was alone, and finding himself crowded by others like him would not change that status: a crowd of Don Giovannis would not make a community.

The same may be said of the present-day successful in secession. The heavily guarded, electronically surveyed 'gated communities' into which the moment they get enough money or credit they buy themselves to keep their distance from the 'messy intimacy' of ordinary city life are 'communities' in name only. What their residents are prepared to pay an arm and a leg for is the right to stay aloof and be free from intruders. 'Intruders' are all other people guilty of having their own agendas and of living their lives in their own ways. The nearness of other agendas and alternative ways of life undermines the comforts of 'finishing quickly and beginning from the beginning' and for this reason 'intruders' are resented as obtrusive and vexing. 'Prowlers' and 'stalkers' are the fear-and-hate figures of the present-day Don Giovannis, and it is freedom from such characters, promised by the heavily armed guards constantly on the beat and a dense network of electronic spy cameras, that makes 'gated communities' so alluring and avidly sought after and becomes a point which the developers and estate agents of such communities emphasize much more than any other feature in their commercial handouts and advertising leaflets.

The world inhabited by the new elite is not however defined by their 'permanent address' (in the old-fashioned physical or topographic sense). Their world has no 'permanent address' except for the e-mail one and the mobile telephone number. The new elite is not defined by any locality: it is truly and fully *exterritorial*. Exterritoriality alone is guaranteed to be a community-free zone, and the new 'global elite' who, except for the inescapable (and occasionally pleasurable) company of maîtres d'hôtels, room-maids and waiters, are its only population wants it to be such a zone.

Respondents to the 'Cultural Globalization Study' conducted by the Institute of Advanced Study in Culture of the University of Virginia,[21] men and women fairly representative of the new exterritorials, entertain no doubts on that point. An AT&T executive avers that he and his co-travellers 'would consider themselves the sort of citizens of the world who happen to carry an American passport'. As the authors of the report conclude from the vast range of responses they have collected, 'they see national boundaries and nation-states as increasingly irrelevant to the main action of life in the twenty-first century.' A Nike executive was quite adamant about his exterritoriality and dismissive of those who think otherwise: 'the only people who will care about national boundaries are politicians.'

Being exterritorial does not mean, though, being a carrier of a new global cultural synthesis, or even establishing links and communication channels between cultural areas and traditions. There is a very narrow, if any, interface between the 'territory of exterritoriality' and the lands in which its various outposts and half-way inns happen to be physically located. As the Virginia researchers point out, the global executives they interviewed

> live and work in a world made up of constant travel between the major global metropolitan centres – Tokyo, New York, London, and Los Angeles. They spend no less than a third of their time abroad. When abroad, most respondents tend to interact and socialize with other 'globalizers' . . . Wherever they go, the hotels, health clubs, restaurants, offices, and airports are all virtually identical. There is a sense in which they inhabit a socio-cultural bubble that is insulated from the harsher differences

between national cultures . . . They are cosmopolitans to
be sure, but in ways that are very limited and insular.

Let's make clear what the authors of the report (and the
authors of numerous other reports by researchers and
journalists, all painting a strikingly similar picture) are
talking about here. Let us ask what the meaning is of that
'cosmopolitanism', the word that tends to be used ever
more often in descriptions of the lifestyle of the 'globaliz-
ers' and in their self-definitions alike? To what sort of
experience and to what cultural traits does this newly
fashionable word refer?

Whatever else the 'cosmopolitanism' of the new global
elite may be, it is *born to be selective*. It is singularly unfit
for the role of a 'global culture': this model cannot be
spread, disseminated, universally shared, used as the stan-
dard-to-be-emulated in a proselytizing/converting mission.
As such, it differs from cultures we know and know of,
those diverse models of 'life decent and proper' which
throughout the modern era used to be held before the
eyes of 'people' by their intellectual leaders, teachers,
moral preachers and other 'reformers' and 'improvers'.
The 'cosmopolitan' lifestyle of the new secessionists is not
meant for mass imitation, and the 'cosmopolitans' are not
the apostles of a new and better life model and not an
avant-garde of an advancing army. What their lifestyle
celebrates is the irrelevance of place, a condition most
conspicuously beyond the reach of ordinary folks, of the
'natives' tied fast to the ground and (in case they try to
disregard the shackles) likely to meet in the 'big wide
world out there' sullen and unfriendly immigration offi-
cers rather than invitingly smiling hotel receptionists. The
message of the 'cosmopolitan' way of being is simple and
blunt: it does not matter *where* we are, what matters is
that *we* are there.

The travels of the new cosmopolitans are not voyages of discovery. Though it is often described as such by the global travellers and their biographers, their lifestyle is not 'hybrid', nor is it particularly notable for its fondness of variety. Sameness is its most conspicuous feature, and it is precisely the worldwide uniformity of pastimes and the globewide similarity of cosmopolitan haunts that the cosmopolitan identity is made up of, and that culturally construes and sustains their collective secession from the variety of natives. Inside the many islands of the cosmopolitan archipelago the public is kept homogeneous, the rules of admission are strict and meticulously (even when informally) enforced, the standards of conduct are precise and exacting and demand unconditional conformity. As in all 'gated communities', the likelihood of meeting a genuine stranger and facing a genuine cultural challenge is reduced to an unavoidable minimum; such strangers as cannot be *physically* removed due to the indispensability of the role they play in servicing the isolation and illusionary 'self-containment' of the cosmopolitan islands are eliminated *culturally*   cast into the background of the 'invisible' and the 'taken for granted'.

More than anything else, the 'bubble' in which the new cosmopolitan business and culture-industry global elite spend most of their lives is – let me repeat – a *community-free zone*. It is a site where a togetherness understood as a sameness (or, more precisely, an insignificance of idiosyncrasies) of casually encountered and 'irrelevant on demand' individuals – and an individuality understood as a trouble-free facility with which partnerships are entered and left – are daily practised to the exclusion of all other socially shared practices. The 'secession of the successful' is, first and foremost, escape from community.

5

Two Sources of Communalism

It seems from this brief survey of the new cosmopolitanism that the successful (those who manage to reforge individuality *de jure*, a *condition* which they share with the rest of modern men and women, into individuality *de facto*, a *capacity* which sets them apart from a great number of their contemporaries) do not need community. There is little they might possibly gain from the tight web of communal obligations, and everything they might lose if caught in that web. In his greatly underrated study composed well before the idea of global hybridity and free-floating cosmopolitans had been invented and made into the folklore of the 'chattering classes',[22] Geoff Dench singled out the feature of community which prompts all those who can afford it to opt out of it: an integral part of the idea of community is the 'fraternal obligation' 'to share benefits among their members, regardless of how talented or important they are'. This feature alone makes 'communalism' 'a philosophy of the weak'. And 'the weak', we may comment, are those individuals *de jure* who are not able to practise individuality *de facto*, and so would fall by the wayside if and when the idea that people deserve what they manage to attain by their own wits and muscles (and deserve no more than that) took over from the obligation of sharing. The idea that merit, and only merit, must be rewarded is readily reworked into a self-congratulatory charter with which the powerful and successful can authorize generous benefits to themselves from social resources. The society open to all talents soon becomes for practical purposes one in which failure to display special ability is treated as sufficient grounds for consignment to a life of submission.

Consignment also, increasingly, to a prospectless misery, as the triumph of meritocratic ideology leads inexorably to its logical conclusion, that is to the dismantling of welfare provisions, that communal insurance against individual misfortune, or to the recasting of such provisions – once seen as a fraternal obligation without discrimination, and a universal entitlement – into a charity on the part of 'those who feel like it' targeted at 'those who need it'.

'The powerful and successful' cannot easily dispose of the meritocratic worldview without seriously affecting the social foundation of the privilege which they cherish and have no intention of surrendering. And as long as that worldview is upheld and made into the canon of public virtue, the communal principle of sharing cannot be accepted. Avarice resulting in a reluctance to reach into one's pocket is not the sole, perhaps not even the principal reason for its non-acceptability. More important things are involved than mere dislike of self-sacrifice: the very principle founding a coveted social distinction is here at stake. If anything other than imputed merit is recognized as a legitimate entitlement to the rewards on offer, that principle would lose its wondrous capacity to bestow dignity on privilege. For the 'powerful and successful', the desire for 'dignity, worth and honour' paradoxically calls for the denial of community.

However true this may be, it is not the whole truth. The 'powerful and successful' may be, *unlike* the weak and the

defeated, resentful of communal bonds – but *like* the rest
of men and women they find life lived in the absence of
community precarious, often dissatisfying and on occasion
frightening. Freedom and communality may clash and
conflict, but a compound lacking one or the other won't
make for a satisfactory life.

The need for both ingredients is, if anything, felt yet
more strongly because life in our fast globalizing and
deregulating society which brought the new cosmopolitan
elite into being, but which has been famously described
by Ulrich Beck as *Risikogesellschaft*, risk society, is a *Risikoleben*, a life of risk – in which 'the very idea of control-
lability, certainty and security . . . collapses';[23] and
because at no other social location has that certainty and
security – and particularly the reassuring feeling of 'knowing for sure what is going to happen' – collapsed so
spectacularly as in the underdefined, underinstitutional-
ized, underregulated and all too often anomic territory of
exterritoriality inhabited by the new cosmopolitans. To
speak of 'collapsing' would perhaps amount to offering
the residual certainty too much credit. It is not as though
the old maps have become outdated and no longer offer
reliable orientation on this unfamiliar ground – it is rather
that ordnance surveys have never been conducted, and
the office that might conduct them has not been established yet, nor is likely to be in the foreseeable future. The
frontierland into which the escape into exterritoriality has
transported the refugees-by-choice has never been
mapped; and there are no permanent features there as yet
fit to be plotted on a map, were one to wish to draw it.
Here, community has not 'been lost'; it was never born.

Here, there is no question of 'denying one's roots' –
there are no roots to be denied. More importantly still,
there is no question here of denying responsibilities to the
weak – there are no weak on this side of the closely

guarded gates, let alone responsibilities for their fate. As a matter of fact, there are no hard-and-fast structures, no class origins one cannot leave behind and no past that refuses to go away or be thrown overboard. Just as it is shapeless and easily overflows any set boundary and any solid mould, the exterritorial habitat of the global elite appears soft and pliable, ready to be rolled out and kneaded by skilful hands. No one stops anyone from being what one is and no one seems to stop anyone from being someone other than one is. Identity appears to be but a matter of choice and resolution, and choices are to be respected and resolution is to be rewarded. Cosmopolitans are born, natural culturalists, culture of their brand of culturalism being an assembly of revocable conventions, the site of invention and experimentation, but above all of no points of no return.

In the book quoted above[24] Richard Rorty writes of the 'cultural Left' in America (a category by and large overlapping with the new cosmopolitan elite under discussion) that came to replace the politically committed Left of the 'great society' era, and whose many members

> specialize in what they call the 'politics of difference', or 'of identity', or 'of recognition'. This cultural Left thinks more about stigma than about money, more about deep and hidden psychosexual motivations than about shallow and evident greed . . . [That 'cultural left'] prefers not to talk about money. Its principal enemy is a mind-set rather than a set of economic arrangements.

It was an undeniable achievement of the new Left to institute (while reflecting upon the 'culturalist' experience and daily practices of their new underdefined habitat) new academic disciplines – like women's history, black, gay, Hispanic-American and other 'victim studies' (as Stefan

Collini generically described them); however, as Rorty caustically observes, the unemployed, homeless or trailer-parks studies are nowhere to be found. It has been left to 'scurrilous demagogues like Patrick Buchanan to take political advantage of the widening gap between rich and poor'.

In the soft and pliable, shapeless world of the global business and culture-industry elite, in which everything can be done and redone while nothing stays tough and solid for long, there is no room for obstinate and stiff realities like poverty, or for that matter for the indignity of being left behind and the humiliation attached to the inability to join in the consumer game. The new elite, with enough private cars not to worry about the sorry state of public transport, indeed drew up behind them the bridges which their parents crossed, but also forgot that such bridges were *socially* built and serviced – and that, had this not have been the case, then they themselves would hardly have landed where they are now.

For all practical intents and purposes, the new global elite have washed their hands of the 'public transport' issue. 'Redistribution' is definitely out, cast into the dust-bin of history among other regrettable errors of judgement which are now retrospectively charged with the oppression of individual autonomy and so with the tapering of that 'space' of which, as we are all fond of repeating, each of us 'needs more'. So out, as well, is community, under-stood as a site of equal shares in jointly attained welfare; as a kind of togetherness which presumes the responsibil-ities of the rich and gives substance to the hopes of the poor that such responsibilities will be taken up.

This is not to say that 'community' is absent from the global elite's vocabulary, or that it is, if spoken about, decried and censured. It is just that the 'community' of the global elite's *Lebenswelt* and that other 'community' of the weak and deprived bear only a very limited resemblance to each other. In each of the two languages in which it appears, the language of the global elite and that of the left-behind, the notion of 'community' collates starkly different life experiences and stands for equally sharply contrasting aspirations.

However much they cherish their individual autonomy, and however confident they might be in their personal and private powers to defend it effectively and to make good use of it, the members of the global elite feel on occasion the need of belonging. Knowing that one is not alone and that one's own personal cravings are shared by others has a reassuring effect. People stumbling from one risky choice to another (we all live, after all, in the *Risikogesellschaft* and living in such a world is a *Risikoleben*), and never quite certain that the choice they make will bring the wholesome results they hope for, won't find a measure of reassurance comes amiss.

In our times, following the devaluation of local opinions and the slow yet relentless demise of 'local opinion leaders' (the issue I discussed more fully in the first two chapters of *Globalization: the Human Consequences*), two authorities and two authorities only are left that are able to endow with a reassuring power the judgements they pronounce or make manifest through their actions: the authority of experts, people 'who know better' (whose area of competence is too vast to be explored and tested by lay people), and the authority of numbers (on the assumption that the larger the numbers, the less likely they are to be wrong). The nature of the first authority makes the exterritorials of the *Risikogesellschaft* into a natural market for the 'counselling boom'. The nature of the second makes them dream of community and gives shape to the community of their dreams.

This community of dreams is an extrapolation of the

identity battles which fill their lives. It is a 'community' of the like-minded and the like-behaving; a community of *sameness* – which, when projected on a wide screen of widely replicated/copied conduct, seems to endow the chosen individual identity with the solid foundations the choosers would not otherwise trust it to possess. When monotonously reiterated by those around, the choices shed much of their idiosyncrasy and no longer appear random, dubious or risky: the security-inspiring solidity which they would badly miss if they stayed unique, they borrow from the imposing heaviness of the mass.

As we have seen before, however, people engaged in identity battles fear ultimate victory more than a string of defeats. The construction of identity is a neverending and forever incomplete process, and must remain such to deliver on its promise (or, more precisely, to keep the promise of delivery credible). In the life politics wrapped around the struggle for identity, self-creation and self-assertion are the main stakes, and freedom to choose is simultaneously the principal weapon and the most coveted prize. Ultimate victory would in one fell swoop remove the stake, decommission the weapon and cancel the prize. To avoid this eventuality, identity must stay *flexible* and always amenable to further experimentation and change; it must be a truly 'until further notice' kind of identity. The facility to dispose of an identity the moment it ceases to satisfy, or is deprived of its allure by competition from other and more seductive identities on offer, is far more vital than the 'realism' of the identity currently sought or momentarily appropriated and enjoyed.

The 'community' whose main uses are to confirm by the impressive power of numbers the propriety of the current choice, and to lend some of its gravity to the identity it stamps with 'social approval', must possess the same traits. It must be as easy to take apart as it has been to put together. It must be and stay flexible, never being more than until further notice and 'as long as the satisfaction lasts'. Its creation and dismantling must be determined by the choices made by those who compose it – by their decisions to bestow or withdraw their allegiance. In no case should the allegiance, once declared, become irrevocable: the bond made by choices should not inconvenience, let alone preclude, further and different choices. The bond sought should not be binding on those who found it. To use Weber's famous metaphors, it is a light cloak, not a steel casing, that is sought.

Such requirements are met by the community of Kant's *Critique of Judgement: the Aesthetic Community*. Identity seems to share its existential status with beauty: like beauty, it has no other foundation to rest on but widely shared agreement, explicit or tacit, expressed in a consensual approval of judgement or in uniform conduct. Just as beauty boils down to artistic experience, the community in question is brought forth and consumed in the 'warm circle' of experience. Its 'objectivity' is woven entirely from the friable threads of subjective judgements, though the fact that they are woven together colours those judgements with a veneer of objectivity.

As long as it stays alive (that is, as long as it is being experienced), aesthetic community is shot through with a paradox: since it would betray or refute the freedom of its members were it to claim non-negotiable credentials, it has to keep its entrances and exits wide open. But were it to advertise the resulting lack of binding power, it would fail to perform the reassuring role which for the faithful was their prime motive in joining it. This is why, as the Czech novelist/philosopher Ivan Klima put it,[25] 'substitute faiths have a limited shelf-life', and 'the more bizarre the belief the more fanatical its adherents'. The less credible are the beliefs expressed by the choices (and so the less likely it is that they will be widely shared, let alone adhered to firmly), the more passion will be needed to put together and to hold together the admittedly vulnerable union of the faithful; and passion being the sole cement holding the company of the faithful together, the 'shelf-life' of the 'community of judgement' is bound to be short. Passions are, after all, notorious for their incurable volatility and the way they shift. The need for aesthetic community, notably the variety of aesthetic community which services the construction/dismantling of identity, tends for those reasons to be as much self-perpetuating as it is self-defeating. That need is never to be gratified, and neither will it ever stop prompting the search for satisfaction.

The need for aesthetic community generated by identity concerns is the favourite grazing ground of the entertainment industry: the vastness of the need goes a long way towards explaining that industry's astonishing, and continuing success.

Thanks to the immense capacities of electronic technology, spectacles can be created which offer a chance of participation and a shared focus of attention to an indefinite multitude of physically remote spectators. Due to the very massiveness of the audience and the intensity of focused attention, the individual finds himself or herself fully and truly 'in the presence of a force which is superior to him and before which he bows'; the condition is thereby met which Émile Durkheim[26] set for the reassuring power of moral guidance designed and enforced by society. The guidance is these days aesthetically, rather than ethically, operated. Its principal vehicle is no longer the ethical authority of leaders with their visions, or moral preachers with their homilies, but the example of 'celebrities in view' (celebrities *because* of being in view); neither the sanctions attached nor their scattered yet rough power of enforcement is its principal weapon. Like all objects of aesthetic experience, the guidance insinuated by the entertainment industry acts through seduction. There are no sanctions against those who fall out of the ranks and refuse to pay attention – apart from their own horror of missing an experience which others (so many others!) relish and enjoy.

The celebrities' authority is a derivative of the authority of numbers – it grows (and falls) together with the number of watchers, listeners, book-buyers or record-buyers. The increase and decrease in their seductive (and hence also reassuring) power are synchronized with the movements of the pendulums of TV ratings and tabloid readership; indeed, the attention paid by TV managers to ratings has a sociological justification deeper than they are aware of. Following the exploits of celebrities is not a matter of idle curiosity or appetite for amusement. The authority of numbers makes the 'individuals in public view' into authoritative examples: it endows their example with added gravity. Indeed, if many people do watch them closely, their example must be 'superior' to what a single spectator on his or her own may learn from his or her own life experience. No wonder that, as Klima quotes from J. G. Ballard's *A User's Guide to the Millennium* (1997),

> interviews crowd the airwaves, a confessional babble only too open to eavesdroppers. At almost any minute of the hour, politicians and film actors, novelists and media celebrities are being relentlessly questioned about their favourite topic, themselves. Many describe their unhappy childhoods, alcoholism and failed marriages with a frankness we would find embarrassing among our closest friends, let alone complete strangers.

What the avid watchers expect to find in the public confessions of the people in the limelight is the reassurance that their own all-too-familiar loneliness is not just liveable, but given some skill and a modicum of luck may be put to good use. But what the spectators who eaves-drop on the celebrities' confessions are rewarded with in the first place is the much missed feeling of belonging: what they are promised day by day ('almost any minute of the hour') is a community of non-belonging, a togeth-erness of loners. Listening to the stories of unhappy childhoods, bouts of depression and broken marriages they are reassured that being alone means being in a big (and widely celebrated) company and that fighting it all alone is what makes them all into a community.

Klima says as well: people nowadays 'need idols to give them a sense of security, permanence and stability in a world that is increasingly insecure, dynamic and change-able'. Yes, they need idols – but to say that they need them for the 'sense of permanence and stability' is Klima's mistake. In a world notoriously 'dynamic and changeable', permanence and stability of the individual, blatantly unshared by those around, would be a recipe for disaster. Idols are needed for another purpose: to give assurance that *non-permanence* and *instability* are not unmitigated disasters, and may prove to be winning tickets in the lottery of happiness; one can make a sensible and enjoy-able life among moving sands. Idols, therefore – such idols as are truly 'needed' – must convey (indeed, embody) the message that impermanence is here to stay while showing that instability is a place to cherish and enjoy. Courtesy of the hype industry, there is no shortage of such idols. Klima lists some of them:

> Footballers, ice-hockey players, tennis players, basketball players, guitarists, singers, film actors, television presenters and top models. Occasionally – and only symbolically – they are joined by some writer, painter, scholar, Nobel

prizewinner (is there anyone who remembers their name a year later?), or princess – her tragic death recalling the ancient tradition of martyrs – until she too is forgotten.

We can see that the selection is by no means random and unmotivated. As Klima himself observes, 'there is nothing quite so transient as entertainment and physical beauty, and the idols that symbolize them are equally ephemeral.' This is, indeed, the crucial point. To serve the purpose, idols must be glittering enough to dazzle the spectators and be formidable enough to fill the stage from wings to wings; but they must be volatile and moveable as well – so they will quickly disappear into the wings of memory and leave the scene free for the crowd of would-be idols waiting their turn. There must be no time for lasting attachments to sediment between the idols and their fans, and particularly no single idol must get a lasting hold. The spectators stay enthralled for what, over the length of their lives, will seem no more than a fleeting moment. The graves of idols early deceased will make the life courses of the spectators like milestones, to be revisited and have flowers laid on them on anniversaries; but it will be up to the spectators, who have since moved on, to recall the deceased from oblivion for one more transient moment. Idols follow the pattern of 'maximal impact and instant obsolescence' which, according to George Steiner, is common to all the cultural inventions of the 'casino culture' of our times.

The idols accomplish a small miracle: they make the inconceivable happen; they conjure up the 'experience of community' without real community, the joy of belonging without the discomfort of being bound. The togetherness *feels real*, is *lived through* as real, yet it is not poisoned by that toughness, resilience and immunity to individual desires which Durkheim believed to be the attributes of reality, but which the mobile residents of exterritoriality abhor and resent as an undue and unbearable invasion of their freedom. Idols, one may say, have been made to order to suit and serviced a life sliced into episodes. The communities which form around them are ready-made, instant communities for on-the-spot consumption – they are also fully disposable after use. These are communities which do not require a long history of slow and painstaking construction, do not need laborious effort to secure their future. For so long as they are being festively and joyfully consumed, idol-centred communities are difficult to distinguish from the 'real stuff' – but compared with the real thing they boast the advantage of being free from the off-putting 'stickiness' and obtrusiveness of the ordinary *Gemeinschaften* with their odious tendency to outlive their usefulness and welcome. The trick which the idol-focused aesthetic communities accomplish is to transform 'community' from a feared adversary of individual freedom of choice into a manifestation and (genuine or illusory) reconfirmation of individual autonomy.

Not all aesthetic communities are idol-centred, to be sure. The pivotal role of the 'celebrity in the limelight' can be played by other entities, notably a true or supposed, but panic-arousing, threat (for instance, by an intention to resettle asylum-seekers close to an established residential area, or by a rumour that supermarket shelves have been stacked with genetically engineered food with unknown consequences for consumers); or by a figure of a 'public enemy' (for instance, by a paedophile released from prison and now at large, or by obtrusive beggars or not-fit-to-be-looked-at homeless vagabonds sleeping rough in public places). Sometimes an aesthetic community may be formed around a one-off recurring festive event – like a pop festival, a football match or a fashionable, much talked about and crowd-pulling exhibition.

Other aesthetic communities are formed around 'problems' with which many individuals are struggling separately and on their own in their daily routine (for instance, weight-watching and inch-fighting); this kind of 'community' comes to life for the duration of the scheduled weekly or monthly ritual, and dissolves again, having reassured its members that tackling individual problems individually while using individual wits and skills is the right thing to do and a thing that all other individuals do with some success and never an ultimate defeat.

All such agents, events and interests providing a focus serve as 'pegs' on which worries and preoccupations which are individually experienced and individually coped with are temporarily hung by a great number of individuals – to be shortly taken off again and hung elsewhere: for that reason aesthetic communities can be described as 'peg communities'. Whatever their focal point, the common feature of aesthetic communities is the superficial and perfunctory, as well as transient, nature of the bonds emerging between their participants. The bonds are friable and short lived. Since it is understood and has been agreed beforehand that they can be shaken off on demand, such bonds also cause little inconvenience and arouse little or no fear.

One thing which the aesthetic community emphatically does not do is to weave between its adherents a web of *ethical responsibilities*, and so of *long-term commitments*. Whatever bonds are established in the explosively brief life of the aesthetic community, they do not truly bind: they are, literally, 'bonds without consequences'. They tend to evaporate at the moment when human bonds truly matter – that is, at a time when they are needed to compensate for the individual's lack of resourcefulness or impotence. Like the attractions on offer in theme parks, the bonds of aesthetic communities are to be 'experienced', and to be experienced on the spot – not taken home and consumed in the humdrum routine of day after day. They are, one may say, 'carnival bonds' and the communities which frame them are 'carnival communities'.

This is not, though, the stimulus which prompts the individuals *de jure* (that is, individuals 'by appointment' – told to resolve their problems by their own cunning for the simple reason that no one else will do it for them), who struggle in vain to become individuals *de facto* (that is, to become masters of their fate in deed, and not merely by public proclamation or self-delusion), to seek a kind of community which could, collectively, make good what they, individually, lack and miss. The community they seek would be an *ethical* community, in almost every respect the opposite of the 'aesthetic' variety. It would need to be woven from long-term commitments, from inalienable rights and unshakeable obligations, which thanks to their anticipated (and better still institutionally guaranteed) durability could be treated as known variables when the future is planned and projects designed. And the commitments which make the community ethical would be of the 'fraternal sharing' kind, reaffirming the right of every member to communal insurance against the errors and misadventures which are the risks inseparable from individual life. In short, what individuals *de jure* but blatantly not *de facto* are likely to read into the vision of community is a warrant of certainty, security and safety – the three qualities they miss most sorely in their life pursuits and which they cannot provide while they are going it alone and relying only on the scarce resources at their private disposal.

These two quite distinct models of community are all too often collapsed together and confused in the currently fashionable 'communitarian discourse'. Once they are collapsed into each other, the salient contradictions that set them apart are misrepresented as philosophical problems and a quandary to be resolved by the refinement of philosophical reasoning – rather than depicted as the products of genuine social conflicts that they really are.

6

Right to Recognition, Right to Redistribution

A most salient characteristic of modernity in its 'solid' state was an *a priori* visualization of a 'final state' which would be the eventual culmination of the current order-building endeavours and at which they would stop – were it a state of a 'stable economy', 'fully equilibrated system', 'just society' or code of 'rational law and ethics'. Liquid modernity, on the other hand, sets the forces of change free, after the pattern of the stock exchange or financial markets: it lets them 'find their own level' and then go on to seek better or more suitable levels – none of the present, and by definition interim, levels is viewed as final and irrevocable. True to the spirit of that fateful transformation, political operators and cultural spokespeople of the 'liquid stage' have all but abandoned the model of social justice as the ultimate horizon of the trial-and-error sequence – in favour of a 'human rights' rule/standard/ measure meant instead to guide the never-ending experimentation with satisfactory, or at least acceptable, forms of cohabitation.

If models of social justice struggled to be substantive and comprehensive, the human rights principle cannot but stay formal and open-ended. The sole 'substance' of that principle is a standing invitation to register old and unfulfilled claims, to articulate new claims and to bid for the recognition of those claims. It is assumed that the question as to which of the indefinite number of rights and which of the many groups and categories of humans clamouring for recognition has been overlooked, neglected, refused recognition or insufficiently catered for is not and cannot be pre-empted or decided in advance. The set of possible answers to this question is in principle never complete and closed, and each currently accepted choice of answers is open to renegotiation; in practice, open to 'reconnaissance battles' – that is, repeated trials of strength meant to reveal just how far back the adversary may be nudged from its present position, how much of its extant prerogatives it may be forced or persuaded to forfeit, and what part of the claim it may be persuaded, compelled or blackmailed to recognize. With all its universalistic ambitions, the practical consequence of the appeal to 'human rights' and the claims to recognition is a setting of ever new battlefronts and a drawing and redrawing of dividing lines along which ever new conflicts will be waged.

As Jonathan Friedman has suggested,[17] we have been landed now in an as yet unexplored world of modernity without modernism: while continuing to be moved by the eminently modern passion for emancipatory transgression, we no longer entertain a clear vision of its ultimate purpose or destination. This is in itself a formidable turnabout: yet more than this has changed, though. The new global power elite, exterritorial and no longer interested in, or downright resentful of the 'engagement on the ground' (particularly a committed, long-term, 'till-death-us-do-part' sort of engagement), has abandoned most, if not all, of the modern elites' ambitions to legislate a new and better order – but it has also lost the once voracious appetite for the administration of order and its day-to-day management. The projects of 'high civilization, high cul-

ture, high science' – converging and unifying in their
intentions if not in practice – are no longer in fashion, and
those cropping up and occasionally aired are treated on a
par with all the other sci-fi products: they are cherished
mostly for their entertainment value and arouse little more
than fleeting interest. As Friedman himself puts it, 'in the
decline of modernism . . . what is left is simply difference
itself and its accumulation.' Of differences, there is no
shortage: 'one of the things that is not happening is that
boundaries are disappearing. Rather, they seem to be
erected on every new street corner of every declining
neighbourhood of our world.'

It is in the nature of 'human rights' that although they
are meant to be enjoyed *separately* (they mean, after all,
the entitlement to have one's own difference recognized
and so to remain different without fear of reprimand or
punishment), they have to be fought for and won *collectively*, and only collectively may they be granted. Hence
the zeal for boundary drawing and for the erection of
closely guarded boundary checkpoints. In order to
become a 'right', difference needs to be shared by a group
or a category of individuals numerous and determined
enough to be reckoned with: it needs to become a stake
in a *collective* vindication of claims. In practice, however,
it all comes down to control of individual movements –
demanding unswerving loyalty from some individuals presumed to be the carriers of the difference for which
recognition is claimed, while barring access to all the
others.

The fight for and the allocation of individual rights
result in intense community-building – in digging trenches
and training and arming assault units: barring intruders
from entry, but also the insiders from getting out; in short,
in a keen control over entry and exit visas. If being and
staying different is a value in its own right, a quality worth

fighting for and preserving at all cost, a clarion call is sounded to enlist, to close ranks and to march in step. First, however, the difference must be found or construed which is fit to be acknowledged as an entitlement to claims falling under the 'human rights' rubric. It is thanks to the combination of all these reasons that the principle of 'human rights' acts as a catalyst triggering the production and self-perpetuation of difference, and the efforts to build a community around it.

Nancy Fraser[28] was therefore right when she protested against the 'widespread decoupling of the cultural politics of difference from the social politics of equality' and insisted that 'justice today required *both* redistribution *and* recognition'.

> It is unjust that some individuals and groups are denied the status of full partners in social interaction simply as a consequence of institutionalized patterns of cultural value in whose construction they have not equally participated and which disparage their distinctive characteristics or the distinctive characteristics assigned to them

For reasons that should be clear by now, the logic of the 'recognition wars' prompts the combatants to absolutize the difference. There is a fundamentalist streak difficult to tone down, let alone to efface, in any recognition claim, and it tends to render the demands for recognition, in Fraser's terminology, 'sectarian'. Placing the issue of recognition in the frame of social justice, instead of the context of 'self-realization' (where, for instance, Charles Taylor or Axel Honneth, in concert with the currently dominant 'culturalist' tendency, prefer to put it) may have a detoxifying effect: it may remove the poison of sectarianism (with all its unprepossessing consequences: physical or social separation, rupture of communication, self-perpetuating and mutually exacerbating hostilities) from the sting of recognition claims. Demands for redistribution voiced in the name of equality are vehicles of integration, while claims to recognition stripped to the bare bones of cultural distinction promote division, separation and in the end a breakdown in dialogue.

Last though not least, reuniting the 'recognition wars' with the demand for equality may also stop the recognition of difference at the very edge of the relativist precipice. Indeed, if 'recognition' is defined as the right to equal participation in social interaction, and if that right is conceived in its turn as a matter of social justice, then it does not follow that (to quote Fraser once more) 'everyone has an equal right to social esteem' (that, in other words, all values are equal and each difference is worthy of cultivation just because of being a difference), but only that 'everybody has an equal right to pursue social esteem under fair conditions of equal opportunity.' When forced into the framework of self-assertion and self-realization and allowed to stay there, recognition wars lay bare their agonistic (and, as recent experience has abundantly confirmed, ultimately genocidal) potential. If, however, they are returned to the problematics of social justice where they belong, recognition claims and the policy of recognition bids become a fertile ground for mutual engagement and meaningful dialogue, which may lead eventually to a new unity – indeed, a widening, rather than a cutting down, of the scope of the 'ethical community'.

All this is not a question of philosophical hair-splitting; it is not as though the philosophical elegance of the argument or the convenience of theorizing were at stake here, and most certainly not them alone. The blend of distributive justice and a policy of recognition is, one may say, a natural sequel to the modern promise of social justice under conditions of 'liquid modernity', or as Jonathan Friedman put it, 'modernity without modernism', which is, as Bruno Latour suggests,[29] the era of reconciliation to the prospect of perpetual coexistence and so a condition which more than anything else needs the art of peaceful and humane cohabitation; an era when hopes can no longer be (or be wished to be) entertained of a one-off and radical eradication of human misery, followed by a conflict-free and suffering-free human condition. If the idea of the 'good society' is to retain its meaning in the liquid modernity setting, it must mean a society concerned with 'giving everyone a chance', and so with the removal of the many impediments to such a chance being taken. We know now that the impediments in question cannot be removed in one fell swoop, through an act of imposition of another, design-built order – and so the sole available strategy through which the postulate of the 'just society' can be met is to eliminate impediments to the equal distribution of chances one by one, as they are revealed and brought to public attention thanks to the articulation, voicing and pursuing of successive recognition claims. Not every difference has the same value, and some ways of life and forms of togetherness are ethically superior to others; but there is no way of finding out which is which unless each one is given an equal opportunity to argue and prove its case. Which form of life will eventually emerge at the far end of negotiation is not a foregone conclusion and cannot be deduced in advance following the rules of philosophers' logic.

'In truth', as Cornelius Castoriadis insisted,[30] 'no problem is resolved in advance. We have to create the good, under imperfectly known and uncertain conditions. The project of autonomy is end and guide, it does not resolve for us effectively actual situations.' We may say that the freedom to articulate and to pursue the claims to recognition is the principal condition of the autonomy, the practical ability of self-constitution (and so, potentially, of self-improvement) of the society we live in; and that it gives us a chance that no injustices and deprivations will be suppressed, covered up, overlooked or otherwise prevented from taking their rightful place in the long line of 'problems' clamouring for resolution. As Castoriadis himself pointed out,

> the alpha and omega of the whole affair is the deployment of social creativity – which, were it unleashed, would once again leave far behind it all we are capable of thinking today . . . To 'reasonably convince' people today means to assist them in attaining their own autonomy.

Castoriadis is at pains to emphasize that he does not 'respect others' difference simply as difference and without regard to what they are and what they do'. Recognition of the 'human right', the right to bid for recognition, is not tantamount to signing a blank cheque and does not mean an *a priori* acceptance of the form of life for which recognition has been or is to be claimed. Recognition of such a right is, instead, an invitation to a dialogue in the course of which the merits and demerits of the difference in question can be discussed and (hopefully) agreed, and so it differs radically not only from the universalist fundamentalism that refuses to recognize the plurality of forms which humanity may take, but also from the kind of tolerance promoted by certain varieties of a so-called 'multiculturalist' policy, which presume the essentialist nature of differences and so also the vanity of negotiation between different ways of life. The standpoint suggested by Castoriadis has to defend its case on two fronts: against engagement taking the form of cultural crusades and oppressive homogenization, on one hand;

and against the lofty and callous indifference of disengagement, on the other.

Whenever the question of 'recognition' is raised, it is because a certain category of people considers itself relatively deprived, and views that deprivation as groundless. As we know from Barrington Moore Jr's classic study of injustice, complaints about deprivation were hardly ever raised in the past just because various categories of people found themselves in unequal conditions (were that the case, the relative paucity of rebellions in most of human history would be a mystery). Low standards of living, however wretched, miserable and repulsive to an outside observer, were as a rule suffered meekly and prompted no resistance if they continued in the same form for a long time and came to be habitualized by the victims as 'natural'. The deprived and the dispossessed rebelled not so much against the dreadfulness of their existence, as against a 'turning of the screw', against being confronted with more demands or being offered fewer rewards than before; in short, not against unsavoury conditions, but against abrupt change in the conditions which they had come to be used to and to endure. The 'injustice' against which they were ready to rebel was measured against their conditions of yesterday, rather than by invidious comparison with other people around.

That rule, operative through most of human history, began to lose its regulative potential with the advent of modernity, and by now it has lost its power altogether. Two aspects of modern life undercut that power more radically than any other changes brought by modernity in its wake.

The first was the proclamation of pleasure, or happiness, as the supreme purpose of life, and the promise made in the name of society and its powers to secure conditions permitting a continuous and consistent growth in the sum total of the pleasure and happiness available. As Harvie Ferguson has suggested,[31] the worldview of the bourgeois, that simultaneously principal character, pace-setter and unwitting scriptwriter of the modern drama of unstoppable and infinite improvement, 'can be under-stood as . . . the pursuit of pleasure', guided by 'regulated insatiability'. Let us note, though, that once it becomes the main objective of life and the measure of its success, the pursuit of pleasure cancels the authority of the past which inclined Barrington Moore Jr's premodern peasant to treat with respect the *Rechtsgewohnenheiten* (old rights, old ways) and to feel obliged to fight if – and only if – the ancient customs were in jeopardy. That the unpleasant-ness is no more than a few days old ceases to be an argument for complacency. There is no longer any point in measuring the justice of one's own condition by reach-ing into memory – there is, however, every reason to compare one's own plight with the pleasures currently on offer, in which other people indulge but which have been denied to oneself. 'Injustice' changes its meaning: it now means being left behind in the universal movement towards a more pleasurable life.

As Jacques Ellul has pointed out,[32]

> In the course of their history, humans fixed for themselves a number of objectives which did not derive from the desire for happiness, and which did not inspire actions aimed at happiness; for instance, as far as the problem of survival, structuration of a social group, play or technical operations or ideology are concerned, the preoccupation with happi-ness does not appear . . . [It was therefore a novelty that the modern revolution proclaimed] the possibility of pro-ducing plenty and so of securing a better material life, an easier life, escaping the dangers, the fatigue, the drudgery, the illnesses, the famine.

Modern society announced the right to happiness: it was not just the improvement in living standards, but the degree of happiness of the men and women involved that was to justify (or to condemn, in the event that that degree refused to climb to ever greater heights) society and all its works. Pursuit of happiness and hope for its success were to become, and to remain, the 'fundamental motivation of the individual's participation in society'. Having been assigned such a role, the pursuit of happiness could not but turn sooner or later from a mere opportunity into a duty and supreme ethical principle. It was now the hurdle accused or suspected of blocking that pursuit which had become the system of injustice and a legitimate cause of rebellion.

The second departure was only to be expected; it could not but follow the axiological revolution under discussion. It concerned the meaning of the 'relative deprivation' which was likely to prompt grievances and remedial action: from *diachronic* (measured against a past condition) it has become *synchronic* (measured against the simultaneous condition of other categories of people). The reference frame in which an unsavoury life condition used to be perceived as 'deprivation', and so unjust (that is, justifying resistance), was the remembered condition which came to be accepted as 'normal'. 'Deprivation' meant a departure from the norm, an abnormality; the present condition must have become worse than the remembered one in order to be seen as a breach of justice. With the advent of modernity, promising a steady increase in happiness, it was however the constancy of living standards and the absence of a visible improvement that could itself be a sign of deprivation; if the standards of other categories of people rose, unlike one's own, or if they rose more quickly and more spectacularly than one's own, a condition that yesterday had been suffered in silence could be recast as a case of deprivation and be felt as a breach of justice. What mattered now was 'income differentials'. Inequality of wealth and income as such could be seen as neither just nor unjust – being merely, like it or not, 'the way things are'; but any widening of the gap between one's own standards and the wealth of those just above, or the closing up or narrowing of the gap separating one's own position from the position of those immediately below offended the feeling of justice and inspired redistributive claims.

Which of the numerous income differentials was to be selected as a benchmark of distributive justice, watched closely and made a site of contention, could not be decided by an objective measure of its size. The decisive factor was the social proximity or distance between differently remunerated categories and the intensity of the interaction between them. As Max Weber indicated,[33] similarity of condition and status did not automatically ensure unified action, just as dissimilarity did not lead necessarily to conflict. For unity and conflict to happen, a mere aggregate of similar units had first to be transformed into a community acting in unison which could then set itself against another group cast as 'the villain of the piece' – either as an object of invidious, yet legitimate comparison or as the agent responsible for the injustices of distribution. 'The fact of identity or similarity of the typical situation in which a given individual and many others find their interests defined' would not suffice to transform a mere similarity of individually suffered deprivation into a community ready to fight for the 'common interest'. Among additional requirements which had to be met for that transformation to occur, Weber names 'the possibility of concentrating on opponents where the immediate conflict of interests is vital', and 'the technical possibility of being easily brought together'. Let us note that both conditions refer to *engagement*: close ties between the members of the emergent 'community of interests' and permanent contact with those presumed to be the threat of such interests.

None of the requirements which according to Weber had to be fulfilled for the 'community of interests' to emerge are met today. To start with, the 'identity or similarity of the typical situation', which Weber could take for granted thanks to the collective bargaining mechanism and collectively signed and collectively binding contracts, can no longer be taken as assured. With the unions disabled as collective subjects and all but incapable of eliciting a sustained concerted action, the 'identity of the typical situation' is anything but self-evident and has ceased to be the prime experience of employees. Remuneration tends to be set individually, promotion and demotions are no longer subject to impersonal rules, career tracks are anything but fixed; under the circumstances, individual competition matters more than joining forces with 'others in similar conditions'.

Most importantly, however, the bonds with the 'others in similar conditions' tend to be fragile and blatantly transient. Tying up and fixing human bonds takes time, and gains from looking to long prospects ahead. Today, however, togetherness tends to be short-term and devoid of prospects – let alone having its future assured. The same applies to the 'opponents on which the conflict of interest might focus'; they are as mobile and volatile as the potential candidates for the union of interests. The would-be community of interests is doomed before it comes together and tends to fall apart before it has had enough time to cement. There are no forces or pressures, either inside or outside, strong enough to keep its boundary in place and to make it into a battleline.

Proximity no longer guarantees intensity of interaction;

most crucially, whatever interaction may emerge on the basis of proximity cannot be trusted to last long, and inscribing individual life expectations into the prospect of its longevity is no longer an obvious or sensible step to take. In the absence of a communal grounding for comparisons, 'relative deprivation' loses much of its meaning and much of the role it played in the evaluation of status and the selection of life strategy. Above all, little has been left of its once powerful community-generating capacity. The perception of injustice and of the grievances it triggers, like so much else in the times of disengagement which define the 'liquid' stage of modernity, has undergone a process of *individualization*. Troubles are supposed to be suffered and coped with alone and are singularly unfit for cumulation into a community of interests which seeks collective solutions to individual troubles.

Once grievances lose their collective character, one may also expect the demise of the 'reference groups' which have served through modern times as the benchmark against which relative deprivation has been measured. This is indeed happening. The experience of life as a thoroughly individual pursuit rebounds in a perception of other people's fortunes or misfortunes as primarily the result of their own industry or indolence, with the addition of a personal stroke of good luck or an individually delivered blow of bad luck ('natural catastrophes', like earthquakes, floods or droughts, being well-nigh the sole exceptions; such exceptions, however, are hardly able to arrest the devaluation of communal action or restore some of its lost value – since by no stretch of imagination can one visualize staving off this kind of disaster by a decision to join forces). Invidious comparisons, if made, tend on the whole to inspire personal envy and enhanced concern with one's own cunning, rather than arouse communal instincts and construe an image of a group conflict of interests.

The collapse of 'reference groups' and the individualization of the idea of relative deprivation has coincided with a spectacular growth in real wealth-and-income differentials unprecedented in the modern era. The gap between the rich and the poor, and the richer and the poorer, widens literally by the year both between and within societies, on a global scale and inside each state unit. In the US, the richest country in the world, and simultaneously the world capital of conflicts of interest and battles for the vindication of claims, the income of bosses of big enterprises in 1999 was 419 times greater than that of manual workers (a mere ten years ago it was only 42 times greater).[34] This is not just a question of the extremes; not a question of a small section of the self-confident global elites awarding themselves benefits no one is strong enough to prevent or revoke, and a somewhat bigger, yet also relatively minor, section of the population at large which has been left out while everyone else has joined an ever more opulent consumer feast. As Richard Rorty points out,[35]

the bourgeoisification of the white proletariat which began in World War II and continued up through the Vietnam War has been halted, and the process has gone into reverse. America is now proletarianizing its bourgeoisie ... The question now is whether the average married couple, both working full time, will ever be able to take home more than $30,000 a year ... But $30,000 a year will not permit homeownership or buy decent daycare. In a country that believes neither in public transportation nor in national health insurance, this income permits a family of four only a humiliating, hand-to-mouth existence. Such a family, trying to get by on this income, will be constantly tormented by fears of wage rollbacks and downsizing, and of disastrous consequences of even a brief illness.

The two developments – the collapse of collective redistribution claims (and more generally, the replacement of the criteria of social justice by those of respect for difference reduced to cultural distinction) and the growth of inequality running wild – are intimately related. There is nothing *incidental* about this *coincidence*. Setting claims for recognition free from their redistributive content allows the growing supply of individual anxiety and fear generated by the precariousness of 'liquid modern' life to be channelled away from the political area – the sole territory where it could crystallize into redemptive action and could therefore be dealt with radically – by blocking its social sources.

When sketching the roads leading from similarity of status to communal action Weber was justified in making a number of tacit assumptions about the nature of the social setting in which the passage takes place and which is necessary for that passage to be possible. Those assumptions, though, can no longer be made: the social setting has changed beyond recognition. One of the most seminal aspects of this change is the emancipation of the 'issue of recognition' from that of redistribution. Claims to recognition tend nowadays to be voiced with no reference to distributive justice. When this happens, tacit assumptions are also made, but unlike the assumptions made by Weber they are counterfactual. What is assumed, after all, is that having legally guaranteed freedom of choice means being free to choose – which, blatantly, is not the case. On the way to the 'culturalist' version of the human right to recognition, the unfulfilled task of the human right to well-being and a life lived in dignity falls by the board.

7

From Equality to Multiculturalism

There seems to be in the contemporary world one prominent exception to the apparently relentless process of
disintegration of the orthodox type of communities: the
so-called 'ethnic minorities'. These seem to retain in full
the ascriptive character of communal membership, the
condition of the community's continuous reproduction.
By definition, though, ascription is not a matter of choice;
and indeed, such choices as mediate the reproduction of
ethnic minorities as communities are the product of
enforcement rather than of freedom to choose and bear
little resemblance to the kind of free decision-making
imputed to the liberated consumer in liberal society.
'Communal values', as Geoff Dench has pointed out,[36]

> revolve around group membership from which there is in
> principle no escape . . . Group membership is ascribed by
> powerful collectivities, onto weaker, with little regard for
> whether there is a subjective basis for the identities
> allocated.

People are assigned to an 'ethnic minority' without
being asked for their consent. They may be glad of the
assignment, or grow to enjoy it and even come to fight for
its perpetuation under a variety of 'black is beautiful'

slogans. The point is, though, that whether this does or does not happen has no tangible influence on the fact of enclosure, which is administered by the 'powerful collectivities' in charge, and perpetuated by the circumstance of their administration. The conditions of cultural separation and of the reduction of cross-culture communication which Robert Redfield considered to be indispensable for a community to form and to survive are therefore met, though not in a way Redfield envisaged when generalizing from his anthropological experience: 'ethnic minorities' are first and foremost products of 'enclosure from outside', and only second, if at all, the outcome of self-enclosure.

'Ethnic minority' is a rubric under which social entities of different types hide or are concealed, and what makes them different is seldom made explicit. The differences do not stem from the attributes of the minority in question, and even less from any strategy the members of the minority may pursue in their conduct. The differences derive from the social context in which they were made into what they are: from the nature of that enforced ascription which led to the enclosure. The nature of the 'greater society' leaves its indelible stamp on every one of its parts.

Arguably the most crucial of the differences dividing the phenomena collated under the generic name of 'ethnic minority' is correlated with the passage from the nation-building stage of modernity to its post nation-state phase.

Nation-building meant the pursuit of the 'one state, one nation' principle, and so ultimately the denial of ethnic diversification among the subjects. From the perspective of the culturally unified and homogeneous 'state nation' the differences in language or custom found on the territory under the state's jurisdiction were but not-yet-fully-extinct relics of the past. The enlightenment or the civilizing processes presided over and monitored by the already unified state powers were designed to ensure that such residual traces of the past wouldn't survive for long. Shared nationhood was to play a crucial legitimizing role in the political unification of the state, and the invocation of common roots and a common character was to be the major tool of ideological mobilization – the production of patriotic loyalty and obedience. That postulate clashed with the reality of variegated languages (now redefined as local or tribal dialects and meant to be replaced by one standard national language), traditions and habits (now redefined as parochialisms and meant to be replaced by one standard historical narrative and standard calendar of memory rituals). 'Local' and 'tribal' meant backwardness; enlightenment meant progress, and progress meant raising the mosaic of ways of life to a common to all, superior level. In practice it meant national homogeneity – and inside the state's borders there was a place for but one language, culture, historical memory and patriotic sentiment.

Nation-building practice had two faces: nationalist and liberal. Its nationalist face was gloomy, cheerless and severe – on occasion cruel, seldom benign. Nationalism was most of the time pugnacious and sometimes gory whenever it encountered a form of life reluctant to embrace the 'one nation' model and eager to stick to its own ways. Nationalism wished to educate and convert, but if persuasion and indoctrination did not work or if their results were slow to come it duly resorted to coercion: the defence of local or ethnic autonomy was criminalized, the leaders of ethnic resistance were proclaimed rebels or terrorists and put in jail or beheaded, speaking 'dialects' in public places or on public occasions was penalized. The nationalist plan to *assimilate* the variety of inherited forms of life and to dissolve them in one national pattern was and had to be power-assisted. As much as the modern state needed nationalist frenzy as the prime legitimation of its sovereignty, nationalism needed a strong state to fulfil its purpose of unification. The state power which nationalism needed had to be free of competitors. All alternative authorities were potentially shelters for sedition. Communities – whether ethnic or local – were prime suspects and the principal enemies.

The liberal face was totally unlike the nationalist one. It was friendly and benevolent; it smiled most of the time, and the smile it wore was inviting. It showed disgust at the sight of coercion and a loathing of cruelty. Liberals refused to force anyone to act against a person's own will, and above all refused to let anyone else do what it abhorred: to impose undesired conversion by force or to prevent, also by force, conversion if conversion was chosen. Again, ethnic and local communities, those conservative forces holding back the individuals eager to self-assert and self-determine, were named the principal culprits and became the main targets in the shooting range. Liberalism believed that if only freedom was refused to the enemies of freedom and the enemies of tolerance were no longer tolerated, the pure essence, common to all humans, would emerge from the dungeons of parochialism and tradition. Nothing would then stand in the way of each one of them freely choosing one loyalty and one identity offered to them all.

For the fate of communities, the choice between the nationalist or liberal faces of the rising nation-state made little difference: nationalism and liberalism might have preferred different strategies, but they shared the same purpose. There was no room for community, and most certainly no room for an autonomous and self-governing community, in either the 'one nation' of the nationalists or the liberal republic of free and unbound citizens.

Whichever of the two faces was looking, it saw the imminent demise of *les pouvoirs intermédiaires*.

The prospect opened up by the nation-building project to ethnic communities was a stark choice: assimilate or perish. Both alternatives pointed ultimately to the same result. The first meant the annihilation of the difference, the second meant the annihilation of the different, but neither allowed for the possibility of the community's survival. The purpose of the assimilatory pressures was to strip the 'others' of their 'otherness': to make them indistinguishable from the rest of the nation's body, to digest them completely and dissolve their idiosyncrasy in the uniform compound of national identity. The stratagem of the exclusion and/or elimination of the allegedly indigestible and insoluble parts of the population had a double function to perform. It was used as a weapon – to separate, bodily or culturally, the groups or categories found to be too alien, too deeply immersed in their own ways or too recalcitrant to change to ever lose the stigma of otherness; and as a threat – to whip up more enthusiasm for assimilation among the lax, the two-minded and the half-hearted.

The choice of fate was not always left to the communities. The decision as to who was and who was not fit for assimilation (and conversely, who was bound to be excluded and prevented from contaminating the national body and sapping the sovereignty of the nation-state) was for the dominant majority, not for the dominated minorities, to take. And to dominate means more than anything else to be free to change one's decisions once they cease to satisfy; to be the source of a constant uncertainty in the condition of the dominated. The decisions of the dominant majority were notorious for their ambiguity and even more for their volatility. Under these circumstances, the choice between an earnest effort to assimilate and rejecting the offer and sticking to one's own separate communal ways come what may was a gamble for the members of the dominated minorities; most of the factors making the difference between success and failure stayed stubbornly beyond their control. In Geoff Dench's words, having been 'suspended in limbo between the promise of full integration and the fear of continuous exclusion', minority individuals would never know

> whether it is realistic to see themselves as free agents in society, or whether it is not better to let official ideology be damned and to congregate with other people sharing the same experience of rejection . . .
>
> This problem of the relative emphasis to give to personal rather than to collective action . . . is made distinctive and more unsettling for minority individuals by the way in which it ties in for them with a second dimension of choice.

Heads, you win; tails, I lose. The promise of equality waiting at the far end of the tortuous and convoluted road to assimilation may be withdrawn at any moment without any reason given. Those who call for the effort sit in judgement over its results, and they are known to be not just demanding but also whimsical judges. Besides, there is a paradox inseparable from any honest effort 'to *become* like them'. 'They' pride themselves on (in fact, define themselves by) having been what they are forever, at least since the ancient act of miraculous creation performed by the Founding Hero of the Nation; to *become* what one *has been* thanks to a long chain of ancestors since times immemorial is fully and truly a contradiction in terms. True, the modern faith allows anyone to become anybody, but one thing it does not permit is to become a somebody who *has never been anybody else*. Even the most zealous and diligent of the voluntary assimilators carry with them into the 'community of destination' the brand of their alien origins, a stigma no oath of loyalty and no leaning over backwards in order to prove its sincerity would ever make non-existent. The sin of the wrong origins – the original sin – may be recalled from oblivion at any stage and made into a charge against the most conscientious and devout 'assimilators'. The test of admission is never final; it cannot be passed conclusively.

There is no evident and risk-free solution to the dilemma that was faced by people declared 'ethnic minorities' by the promoters of the nation's unity. In addition, were those who took up the offer of assimilation to cut their ties with their native community and turn their backs on their former brethren to prove their unswerving loyalty to their new brothers-by-choice they would immediately become suspected of the morbid vice of turncoating disloyalty and so of being types who could not be trusted. Were they, on the other hand, to engage in community work in order to help their brothers-by-birth to lift themselves collectively from collective inferiority and collectively suffered discrimination, they would immediately stand accused of two-facedness and duplicity, and asked: which side are you on?

In some perverse sense it may therefore be better, even more humane, to be declared unfit for assimilation from the start and so be denied the choice. True, a lot of suffering would follow such a declaration, but a lot of suffering would be spared. The torment of risk, the fear of embarking on a journey that may prove without issue but also without return, is the greatest of the sufferings escaped by a 'minority' which has been explicitly denied an invitation to join the nation, or, if the invitation was extended, has seen it unmasked at an early stage as a false promise.

'Communalism' comes most naturally to the people

summarily denied the right to assimilation. They have been denied the choice – seeking a shelter in the assumed 'fraternity' of the native group is their only option. Voluntarism, individual freedom, self-assertion are all synonyms of the emancipation from communal ties, of the capacity to disregard the inherited ascription – and this is precisely what they have been deprived of by the non-issuing or withdrawal of the offer of assimilation. Members of 'ethnic minorities' are not 'natural communalists'. Their 'really existing communalism' is power-assisted, the result of expropriation. The property not allowed or the property taken away is the right to choose. All the rest follows from that primary act of expropriation; at any rate, it would not happen if the expropriation did not occur. The decision of the dominant to enclose the dominated in the shell of an 'ethnic minority' on the grounds of its reluctance or unfitness to break the shell has all the marks of a self-fulfilling prophecy.

To quote Dench once more:

> fraternalist values are inescapably hostile to voluntarism and individual freedom. They have no valid conception of natural and universal man . . . The only human rights which can be admitted are those logically attendant on duties to the collectivities providing them.

Individual duties cannot be merely contractual; the no-choice situation into which the act of summary exclusion has cast the 'ethnic minority' rebounds in a no-choice situation for the individual members when it comes to their communal duties. A common response to the rejection is a 'besieged fortress' spirit, which denies to those inside all options except unconditional loyalty to the common cause. It will be not just an explicit refusal to assume the communal duty that will be branded as treason, but a less than full dedication to the communal cause. A sinister 'fifth column' conspiracy is spied in every sceptical gesture and every question addressed to the wisdom of communal ways. The half-hearted, the lukewarm, the indifferent become the community's prime enemies; the main battles are fought on the domestic front rather than on the ramparts of the fortress. The declared fraternity reveals its fratricidal face.

In the case of summary exclusion, no one can easily opt out of communal enclosure; the rich and resourceful have, like everyone else, nowhere to go. This circumstance adds to the resilience of the 'ethnic minority' and gives it a survivalist edge over communities which have not been barricaded out from the 'greater society' and which tend to dissipate and lose their distinctiveness much more quickly, being promptly deserted by their native elites. But it also brings further cuts in the freedom of community members.

Many causes combined to render the two-pronged strategy of nation-building unrealistic. More reasons yet allied to render the application of that strategy less urgent, less eagerly sought or downright undesirable. Accelerated globalization is arguably the 'metareason', a departure from which all other reasons follow.

More than anything else, 'globalization' means that the network of dependencies is fast acquiring a worldwide scope – a process which is not being matched by a similar extension of viable institutions of political control and by the emergence of anything like a truly global culture. Closely intertwined with the uneven development of economy, politics and culture (once coordinated in the framework of the nation-state) is the separation of power from politics: power, as embodied in the worldwide circulation of capital and information, becomes exterritorial, while the extant political institutions stay, as before, local. This leads inevitably to the progressive disempowerment of the nation-state; no longer able to muster enough resources to balance the books effectively and to conduct an independent social policy, the governments of states have little choice except to pursue a strategy of deregulation: that is to surrender control over economic and cultural processes and to cede it to the 'powers of the market', that is to essentially exterritorial forces.

An abandonment of that normative regulation that was once a trademark of the modern state renders the cultural/ideological mobilization of the subject population, once the modern state's principal strategy, and the evocation of nationhood and patriotic duty, once its main legitimation, redundant: they serve no visible purpose. The state no longer presides over the processes of social integration or systemic management which made normative regulation, management of culture and patriotic mobilization indispensable, leaving such tasks (by design or default) to forces over which it has no effective jurisdiction. The policing of the administered territory is the sole function left entirely in the hands of state governments; other orthodox functions have been either renounced or have come to be shared and so are only in part, and not autonomously, monitored by the state and its organs.

This transformation, however, deprives the state of its past status as the paramount, perhaps the only seat of sovereign power. Nations, once securely ensconced in the armoury of the multidimensional sovereignty of the nation-state, have found themselves in an institutional void. Existential security has been shattered; the old stories reiterated to replenish the confidence of belonging are losing growing amounts of their credibility, and as Jeffrey Weeks has indicated in another context,[37] when the old stories of group (communal) belonging no longer ring true, demand grows for the 'identity stories' in which 'we tell ourselves about where we came from, what we are now and where are we going'; such stories are urgently needed to restore security, build trust and make 'meaningful interaction with others possible'. 'As the old certainties and loyalties are swept away people seek new belongings.' The trouble with new identity stories, in sharp distinction from the old stories of 'natural belonging' verified daily by the seemingly invulnerable solidity of deeply entrenched institutions, is that 'trust and commitment have to be worked at in relationships that no one dictates should last unless individuals choose to make them last.'

The normative void opened by the withdrawal of pernickety state regulation undoubtedly brings more freedom. No 'identity story' is immune to corrections; it can be recanted if found unsatisfactory or not as good as the next. In the void, experimentation is easy and meets few obstacles – but the snag is that, whether enjoyable or not, the experimental products are never secure; their life expectation is admittedly short and so the existential security they promised to bring back is reluctant to arrive. If relationships (including communal togetherness) have no other guarantee of durability than the individuals' choices 'to make them last', the choices need to be repeated daily, and be manifested with a zeal and dedication which would make them truly hold. The chosen relationships won't last unless the will to hold them is protected against the danger of dissipation.

This is not a major tragedy (it may even be good news) for the resourceful and self-reliant individuals who count on their own ability to stem the adverse tides and protect their choices from being swept away, or failing that, to make new choices, different, yet no less satisfactory. Such individuals feel no urge to seek a communal warrant for their security, given the price-tag carried by all long-term commitments (and so a communal membership which neither at the point of entry nor at the point of exit allows for free choice). It is different for the individuals who are neither resourceful nor self-reliant. To such individuals, the suggestion that the collectivity in which they seek shelter and from which they expect protection has a more solid foundation than notoriously capricious and volatile individual choices is exactly the kind of news they want to hear. The price-tag attached to an involuntary, lifelong belonging that allows no termination-on-demand does not look sinister at all, given that what has been denied – the right to a free choice of identity – was in the case of weak and resourceless individuals an illusion all along, and, to add insult to injury, also a cause of perpetual self-depre-cation and public humiliation.

Therefore, as Jeffrey Weeks points out,

> The strongest sense of community is in fact likely to come from those groups who find the premises of their collective existence threatened and who construct out of this a com-munity of identity which provides a strong sense of resist-ance and empowerment. Seeming unable to control the social relations in which they find themselves, people shrink the world to the size of their communities and act politi-cally on that basis. The result, too often, is an obsessive particularism as a way of embracing or coping with contingency.

Recasting quite real individual frailties and infirmities into the (imagined) potency of community results in conservative ideology and exclusivist pragmatics. Conser-vatism ('going back to the roots') and exclusivism ('they' are, collectively, a threat to 'us', collectively) are indis-pensable if the word is to become flesh, if the imagined community is to spawn the network of dependencies that would make it real, and if W. I. Thomas's famous rule 'if people define a situation as real, it tends to become real in its consequence' is to operate.

The sad truth is that the overwhelming majority of the population orphaned by the nation-state when it renounced, one by one, its security-and-confidence-generating functions belongs to the 'frail and infirm' category. We are all asked, as Ulrich Beck observed, to 'seek biographical solutions to systemic contradictions', but only a small minority of the new exterritorial elite may boast of finding them, or, if they haven't found them yet, of being fully capable of finding them in the nearest future. Seeking with a near certainty of finding is a pleasurable pastime, and the not-finding-as-yet or the found to be wrong-this-time adds, if anything, excitement to the long voyage of discovery. Seeking with a near certainty of failure is, however, a harrowing experience – and so a promise to relieve the seekers of the obligation to go on searching sounds sweet. One needs, following Odysseus' example, to plug one's ears tightly not to fall victim to the sirens' song.

We live in times of great and growing globewide migration. Governments strain their ingenuity to the utmost in order to ingratiate themselves with the electors by tightening the immigration laws, restricting the rights to asylum, blackening the image of 'economic migrants' who, unlike the electors encouraged to mount their bikes in search of economic bliss, happen also to be foreigners – but there is little prospect that the 'great migration of nations mark two' will grind to a halt. Governments and the lawyers they hire lean over backwards to draw a line between the free circulation of capital, finance, investments and the businesspeople who carry them, welcoming them and wanting them to multiply and the transmigrations of the job-seekers which they, not to be outdone by their electors, publicly abhor – but such a line cannot be drawn and, if drawn, would be promptly obliterated. There is a point at which the two intentions clash with each other; freedom of trade and investment would soon reach its limits if it were not complemented by the right of job-seekers to go where the jobs are waiting to be filled.

There is no denying the fact that those exterritorial free-floating 'market forces' are instrumental in setting the 'economic migrants' on the move. Yet the territorial governments, however reluctantly, find themselves time and again obliged to cooperate. Jointly, the two forces promote the processes which one of them at least would otherwise dearly wish to arrest. According to Saskia Sassen's study,[38] whatever their spokespeople may say, the actions of exterritorial agencies and local governments prompt even more intense migration. People with no income and little hope left after the devastation of traditional local economies are easy prey for semi-official, semi-criminal organizations specializing in 'trafficking in humans'. (In the 1990s criminal organizations earned an estimated 3.5 billion dollars a year from illegal migration – though not without governments offering tacit support or turning their eyes the other way. If, for instance, the Philippines tried to balance their books and pay back part of the governmental debt through the official export of their surplus population, US and Japanese authorities passed laws allowing the import of foreign workers in trades suffering an acute shortage of labour.)

The sediment of the combined pressures is a globewide spread of ethnic diasporas; people remain much less volatile than the cycles of economic boom and depression, and the history of past cycles leaves behind a long and wide trail of immigrants struggling to settle. Even if they wished to embark on another journey and leave, the same policy contradictions which brought the immigrants 'in' would prevent them from acting on their wishes. The immigrants have no choice but to become another 'ethnic minority' in the country of arrival. And the locals have no choice but to brace themselves for a long life amidst diasporas. Both are expected to find their own ways of coping with the power-assisted realities.

As a conclusion to his comprehensive study of one of these diasporas in Britain, Geoff Dench suggests that

> Many people in Britain . . . do regard ethnic minorities as outsiders whose destinies and loyalties are self-evidently divergent from those of British people, and whose dependent and inferior standing in Britain goes without saying. Wherever a conflict of interests arises it is axiomatic that public sympathy should be against them . . .[39]

This, obviously, does not apply only to Britain and only to one (Maltese) 'ethnic minority', the focus of Dench's study. The reported attitudes have been recorded in every country with sizeable diasporas, and that means virtually the whole of the globe. The proximity of 'ethnic strangers' triggers ethnic instincts in the locals, and the strategies that follow such instincts are aimed at the separation and ghettoization of 'alien elements', which in turn reverberate in the impulse to self-estrangement and self-enclosure of the forcefully ghettoized group. The process has all the markings of Gregory Bateson's 'schismogenetic chain' known for its propensity for self-perpetuation and notoriously difficult to arrest, let alone cut. And so the tendency to communal enclosure is prompted and encouraged in both directions.

Much though the liberally minded opinion-makers may bewail this state of affairs, there seem to be no political agents in sight genuinely interested in breaking the vicious circle of mutually reinforcing exclusivities, let alone working in practice to eliminate their sources. On the other hand, many of the most potent forces conspire, or at least act in unison, to perpetuate the exclusivist trend and the building of barricades.

First, there is the old and well-tried *divide et impera* principle to which powers of all eras have gladly resorted whenever they have felt threatened by the collation and condensation of the otherwise varied and dispersed grievances and discontents. If only one could prevent the anxieties and angers of the sufferers from flowing into one riverbed, if only the many and different oppressions could be suffered by each category of the oppressed separately, then the tributaries could be diverted and the energy of protest dissipated and soon used up in a plethora of intertribal and intercommunal enmities – with the powers at the top assuming the roles of impartial judge, promoter of equality between the clashing claims, defender of the peace and saviour and benevolent protector of each and every side in the internecine war; their role in bringing about the conditions which made the war all but inevitable would be conveniently overlooked or forgotten. Richard Rorty[40] offers a 'thick description' of the present-day uses of the ancient divide et impera strategy:

> The aim will be to keep the bottom 75 percent of Americans and the bottom 95 percent of the world's population busy with ethnic and religious hostilities . . . If the proles can be distracted from their own despair by media-created pseudo-events, including the occasional brief and bloody war, the super-rich will have nothing to fear.

When the poor fight the poor, the rich have every reason to rejoice. It is not only that the prospect that the sufferers will sign a pact against the culprits responsible for their misery becomes infinitely remote, as it was in the past whenever the *divide et impera* principle was successfully applied. There are less banal reasons to rejoice – reasons specific to the new character of the global power hierarchy. As has already been indicated, this new hierarchy is operated by a strategy of disengagement which in its turn depends on the ease and speed with which the new global powers are able to move, cutting themselves off from their local commitments at will and without notice and leaving to the 'locals' and all those left behind the awesome task of cleaning up the debris. The elite's freedom to move depends to a very great extent on the locals' inability or unwillingness to get their act together. The more pulverized they are, the weaker and more minute the units into which they are split, the more their wrath is expended on fighting their similarly impotent neighbours next door, the smaller is the chance that their act will ever be got together. No one will ever be strong enough to prevent another vanishing act, to stem the flow, to hold in place the volatile resources of survival. Contrary to a frequently voiced opinion, the absence of political agencies able to match the scope of economic powers is not a matter of developmental lag; it is not as though the extant political institutions have not as yet had enough time to combine into a new global system of democratically controlled checks and balances. It seems, on the contrary, that the pulverization of public space and its saturation with intercommunal strife is precisely the kind of political 'superstructure' (or should we now call it 'understructure'?) that the new power hierarchy serviced by the strategy of disengagement needs and would openly or surreptitiously cultivate if allowed to do so. Global order needs a lot of local disorder 'to have nothing to fear'.

In the last quotation from Rorty I left out a reference to 'debates about sexual mores' as another factor alongside 'ethnic and religious hostilities' responsible for the 'super-rich' 'having nothing to fear'. This was a reference to the 'culturalist left' which, for all its merits in fighting a sadistic intolerance to cultural otherness widespread in American society, is, in Rorty's opinion, guilty of effacing the question of material deprivation, the deepest source of all inequality and injustice, from the public agenda. Sexual mores were no doubt exploited as one of the more important footholds for intolerance – the point is, though, that if attention is focused on civility and political correctness in encounters with difference of mores, it will have little chance of digging deeper into the roots of inhumanity. It will do more damage than that: it will absolutize the difference and bar all debate about the relative virtues and demerits of coexisting forms of life. The small print is that all differences are good and worth preserving just for the fact of being different; and all debate, however serious, honest and civil, is to be put out of bounds in case it is aimed at reconciling the extant differences so that the overall standards binding human life can be lifted to a higher (and presumably better) level. Jonathan Friedman dubbed the intellectuals holding such views as 'modernists without modernism' – that is, thinkers bent, in the hallowed modernist tradition, on transcendence, but deprived of any idea of the destination to which the transcendence may (or should) eventually lead and shunning all advance consideration of its shape. The outcome is an unwitting contribution to the perpetuation, even the acceleration of the current pulverizing tendency; it makes it all the more difficult for a serious cross-cultural dialogue to take place, the only action which could overcome the current incapacitating fissiparousness of the potential political agents of social change.

The attitudes to which both Rorty and Friedman refer are not really surprising. One may say that this is exactly what one would expect from a knowledge elite which opted out from its modern role of enlighteners, guides and teachers and followed (or were pushed to follow) the lead of the other, business, sector of the global elite into the new strategy of detachment, distantiation and non-commitment. It is not so much that the present-day knowledge classes have lost their faith in progress and grown suspicious of all advance models of progressive transformation; a more important reason for embracing the disengagement strategy was, it seems, an abhorrence of the immobilizing impact of long-term commitments and of the cumbersome and messy ties of dependency which the now abandoned alternative would inevitably have entailed. Like so many of their contemporaries, the descendants of modern intellectuals want, and seek, 'more space'. Engagement with 'the other', unlike 'letting the other be', would cut into that space instead of adding to it.

The new indifference to difference is theorized as recognition of 'cultural pluralism': the policy informed and supported by that theory is 'multiculturalism'. Ostensibly, multiculturalism is guided by the postulate of liberal tolerance and by care for the communities' right to self-assertion and public recognition of their chosen (or inherited) identities. It works, though, as an essentially conservative force: its effect is a recasting of inequalities, which are unlikely to command public approval, as 'cultural differences' – something to cherish and obey. The moral ugliness of deprivation is miraculously reincarnated as the aesthetic beauty of cultural variety. What has been lost from view in the process is that the bid for recognition is toothless unless sustained by the practice of redistribution – and that the communal assertion of cultural distinctiveness brings little consolation for those who, courtesy of the increasingly unequal division of resources, have their 'choices' made for them.

Alain Touraine[41] has proposed that 'multiculturalism'

as a postulate of respect for freedom of cultural choices amidst a variety of cultural offers be set apart from something sharply different (if not outspokenly, then at least in its consequences): a vision better called *multicommunitarianism*. The first demands respect for the right of individuals to select their modes of life and their allegiances; the second assumes, on the contrary, that the individual's allegiance is an open-and-shut case, settled by the fact of communal belonging and so better left out of negotiation. Confusing the two strands in the multiculturalist credo is, however, as common as it is misleading and politically harmful.

As long as that confusion lasts, 'multiculturalism' plays into the hands of politically unconstrained globalization; the globalizing forces are allowed to get away with their devastating consequences, among which rampant intersocietal and intrasocietal inequalities loom larger than any. The former blatantly arrogant habit of explaining inequality by an inborn inferiority of races has been replaced by an apparently humane representation of starkly unequal human conditions as the inalienable right of every community to its own chosen form of life. The new culturalism, like the old racism, aims to placate moral scruples and produce reconciliation with the fact of human inequality either as a condition beyond the capacities of human intervention (in the case of racism) or as a plight which humans should not interfere with lest sacrosanct cultural values be violated. The obsolete, racist formula of reconciliation with inequality was closely associated with the modern search for the 'perfect social order': each order-building necessarily involves selection, and it stood to reason that inferior races incapable of eking out decent human standards would find no room in any order approximating perfection. The new culturalist formula is, for a change, intimately related to the abandonment of 'good society' blueprints. If no revision of social arrangements is on the cards – either dictated by historical inevitability or suggested by ethical duty – then it stands to reason that everyone is entitled to seek one's place in the fluid order of reality and bear the consequences of the choice.

What the 'culturalist' worldview leaves unsaid is that inequality is its own most potent cause, and that representing the divisions it spawns as an inalienable aspect of, rather than a paramount obstacle to, freedom of choice is one of the principal factors in its self-perpetration.

There are some other problems to look into, though, before we return to the scrutiny of 'multiculturalism' in the last chapter.

8

The Bottom Line: the Ghetto

A bizarre adventure happened to space on the road to globalization: it lost its importance while gaining in significance. On one hand, as Paul Virilio insists,[42] territorial sovereignty has lost almost all substance and a good deal of its former attraction: if every spot can be reached and abandoned instantaneously, a permanent hold over a territory with its usual accompaniment of long-term duties and commitments turns from an asset into a liability and becomes a burden rather than a resource in a power struggle. On the other hand, as Richard Sennett points out,[43] 'as the shifting institutions of the economy diminish the experience of belonging somewhere special . . . people's commitments increase to geographic places like nations, cities and localities.' On one hand, everything can be done to faraway, other people's places, without going anywhere. On the other, little can be prevented from being done to one's own place, however vigilantly and stubbornly one tries to hold one's ground.

As far as the daily experience shared by most of us is concerned, a particularly poignant consequence of the new global network of dependencies combined with the gradual, yet relentless dismantling of the institutional safety-net which used to protect us from the vagaries of the market and the caprices of a market-concocted fate is paradoxically (though psychologically speaking not at all surprisingly) the *increased value of place*. As Richard Sennett explains that paradox, 'the sense of place is based on the need to belong not to "society" in the abstract, but to somewhere in particular; in satisfying that need, people develop commitment and loyalty.' The abstractness of 'society', let me add, might have been society's constant feature, but nowadays it is ever more evident and acutely felt.

It is true that 'society' was always an *imagined* entity, never given to experience in its totality; not so long ago, however, its image was one of a 'caring-and-sharing' community. Through welfare provisions seen as the birthright of the citizen rather than a charitable hand-out for the less capable, invalid or indolent, that image radiated a comforting trust in a collective insurance against individual misfortune. Society was imagined after the pattern of a powerful father, stern and sometimes unforgiving, but a father nevertheless, someone to whom one could confidently turn for help in case of trouble. Having since shed, or having been robbed of many of the effective tools for action it wielded in the times of the nation-state's uncontested sovereignty, 'society' has, however, lost a good deal of its 'paternal' resemblance. It may still cause hurt on occasion, and painfully; but when it comes to the supply of goods necessary for a decent life and for fighting back against the adversities of fate, it looks disconcertingly empty-handed. No wonder that any hopes of salvation that may descend from the (properly manned) control towers of 'society' wilt and fade. No wonder either that the 'good society' is a notion most of us would not bother thinking about, and that many would think such thinking to be a waste of time.

Frustrated love ends in indifference at best, but more often than not in suspicion and resentment. If 'society' does not satisfy the desire for a secure home, it is not so much because of its 'abstractness' (it is no more abstract or 'imaginary', let us remember, than 'nation' or any other contemporary 'communities') as because of its recent treachery still fresh in popular memory. It has not delivered on its promises; from the most vital of its promises it has openly retreated. To people who are smarting under the pressures of an insecure existence and uncertain prospects, it promises more, not less insecurity: in a drastic change of tune still difficult to assimilate, its spokespeople call for more 'flexibility'; they admonish individuals to exercise their own wits in the search for survival, improvement and a dignified life, to rely on their own guts and stamina and blame their own lassitude or laziness in the event that they suffer defeat.

Among the imagined totalities to which people were able to believe they belonged and where they believed they could seek (and hopefully find) shelter, a void yawns at the spot once occupied by 'society'. That term once stood for the state, armed with means of enforcement as well as with powerful means of rectifying at least the most outrageous of social injustices. Such a state is receding from view. To hope that the state, if properly asked or pressed, would do something tangible to mitigate the insecurity of existence is not much more realistic than the hope of ending the drought by a rain-dance. It looks increasingly likely that the missing comforts of a safe existence need to be sought through other means. Safety, like all other aspects of human life in a relentlessly individualized and privatized world, must be a 'do-it-yourself' job. 'Defence of the place', seen as the necessary condition of all safety, must be a neighbourhood matter, a 'communal affair'. Where the state has failed, perhaps the community, the *local* community, the physically tangible, 'material' community, a community embodied in a *territory* inhabited by its members and no one else (no one who 'does not belong'), will purvey the 'being safe' feeling which the wider world evidently conspires to destroy?

The place as such might have lost its importance for the flying elite, now able to view all places with detachment and from a distance, after a fashion once considered to be the privilege of birds. But even the members of the globe-trotting elite need breaks in the harrowing, nerve-straining voyages, times to disarm and rest, to replenish their depleting power to resist daily tension – and for this purpose they need a secure place of their own. Perhaps the other places, other people's places, do not matter – but that special place, their own place, does. Perhaps also the knowledge of how pliable and indefensible the places of other people tend to be adds urgency to the need to fortify, make foolproof and impregnable that one special place of one's own.

Certainty and security of existential conditions can hardly be bought by drawing on one's own bank account – but the safety of place can if only the account is large enough; the bank accounts of the 'globals' are as a rule sufficiently large. The globals can afford the safety indus-try equivalents of *haute couture*. The rest, no less tor-mented by the gnawing sense of the world's unbearable volatility yet themselves not volatile enough to surf the waves, have as a rule fewer resources and must settle for inferior mass-production replicas of the high fashion art. That rest can do even less, in fact next to nothing, to mitigate the uncertainty and insecurity endemic in the world they inhabit – but they can invest their last pennies in the safety of their bodies, their possessions, their street. Not that long ago people who believed that nuclear con-frontation could not be stopped sought rescue in building family nuclear shelters. People who believe that nothing can be done to tone down, let along to exorcise, the spectre of insecurity are busy shopping for burglar alarms and barbed wire. What they are after is an equivalent of a personal nuclear shelter; the shelter they are after they call 'community'. The 'community' they seek stands for a burglar-free and stranger-proof 'safe environment'. 'Community' stands for isolation, separation, protective walls and guarded gates.

Sharon Zukin describes, after Mike Davis's *City of Quartz* (1990), public spaces in Los Angeles as they have been reshaped by the safety concerns of the residents and their elected or appointed custodians: 'Helicopters buzz the skies over ghetto neighbourhoods, police hassle teen-agers as putative gang members, homeowners buy into the type of armed defense they can afford . . . or have nerve enough to use.' The 1960s and early 1970s were, Zukin says, 'a watershed in the institutionalization of urban fear':

> Voters and elites – a broadly conceived middle class in the United States – could have faced the choice of approving government policies to eliminate poverty, manage ethnic competition, and integrate everyone into common public institutions. Instead, they chose to buy protection, fuelling the growth of the private security industry.

A most tangible danger to what she calls 'public culture' is found by Zukin in 'the politics of everyday fear'. The blood-curdling and nerve-wracking spectre of 'unsafe streets' keeps people away from public spaces and turns them away from seeking the art and the skills needed to share in public life.

> 'Getting tough' on crime by building more prisons and imposing the death penalty are all too common answers to the politics of fear. 'Lock up the whole population,' I heard a man say on the bus, at a stroke reducing the solution to its ridiculous extreme. Another answer is to privatize and

militarize public space – making streets, parks, and even shops more secure but less free . . .[44]

Safe neighbourhood visualized as armed gatekeepers controlling the entry; stalker and prowler, who have come to replace the early modern bugbear of *mobile vulgus,* jointly promoted to the rank of new public enemies number one; a paring down of public areas to 'defensible' enclaves with selective access; separation in lieu of the negotiation of life in common; the criminalization of residual difference – these are the principal dimensions of the current evolution of urban life. And it is in the cognitive frame of this evolution that the new notion of 'community' is formed.

According to that notion, community means *sameness,* while 'sameness' means the absence of the Other, especially a stubbornly *different* other capable of a nasty surprise and mischief precisely by reason of their difference. In the figure of the stranger (not just the 'unfamiliar', but the *alien,* the 'out of place'), the fears of uncertainty, founded in the totality of life experience, find their eagerly sought, and so welcomed, embodiment. At long last, one won't feel humiliated for taking the blows without raising one's hands – one can do something real and tangible to parry the random blows of fate, perhaps even foil them or ward them off. Given the intensity of fears, were there no strangers they would have to be invented. And they are invented, or rather construed, daily: by neighbourhood watch, closed-circuit TV, hired guards armed to the teeth. Vigilance and the defensive/ aggressive exploits it triggers create their own object. Thanks to them, the stranger is transmogrified into an alien, and the alien into a threat. The scattered, free-floating anxieties acquire a hard nucleus. The age-old dream of purity, not so long ago wrapped around the vision of the 'perfect' (transparent, predictable, free from contingency) society, now has 'safe neighbourhood community' as its prime object. What looms therefore on the horizon of the long march towards 'safe community' (community *as* safety) is a bizarre mutant of a 'voluntary ghetto'.

A ghetto, as Loïc Wacquant defines it,[45] combines spatial confinement with social closure: we may say that the phenomenon of the ghetto manages to be simultaneously territorial and social, by blending the *physical* proximity/ distance with *moral* proximity/distance (in Durkheim's terms, it collapses moral density with physical density). Both 'confinement' and 'closure' would carry little substance were they not complemented with a third element: *homogeneity* of those inside contrasted with the *heterogeneity* of the outside. Throughout the long history of the ghetto, as well as in the American black ghetto, its present-day archetypal specimen, that third element has been supplied by ethno-racial division. It takes a similar form in the numerous 'immigrant ghettos' scattered over European and American cities. It is only the ethnic/racial division that gives the homogeneity–heterogeneity opposition the capacity to infuse the ghetto walls with the kind of solidity, durability and reliability they need (and are needed for). For this reason, the ethnic/racial division is a natural 'ideal pattern' to be followed by all other 'second best', substitute divisions pretending to play the role of the third element, the homogeneity/heterogeneity division, a model they try hard to emulate and whose feathers they are eager to steal.

'Voluntary ghettos' are not true ghettos, of course, and they have their volunteers (that is, they may tempt and arouse desire, prompting people to construe their mock replicas) precisely because they are not the 'real thing'. Voluntary ghettos differ from true ghettos in one decisive respect. The real ghettos are places from which their insiders cannot get out (as Wacquant puts it, the residents of American black ghettos 'cannot casually cross over into adjacent white neighbourhoods, for . . . they will promptly be trailed and stopped, nay systematically harassed, by police'); the prime purpose of voluntary ghettos, on the contrary, is to bar outsiders from going in – the insiders are free to go out at will.

True, the people who pay an arm and a leg for the privilege of 'spatial confinement and social enclosure' are zealous in justifying the investment by painting the wilderness outside the gates in the blackest of colours, just as it may appear to the involuntary residents of real ghettos. No argument would however inspire the choosers of ghetto-like enclosures to lock the gates were it not for soothing awareness that there is nothing final and revocable about the decision to buy a house inside the quasi-ghetto walls. The real ghettos mean denial of freedom. Voluntary ghettos are meant to serve the cause of freedom.

Their suffocating effect is 'an anticipated consequence' – it has not been intended. The inhabitants find to their dismay that the safer they feel inside the enclosure, the less familiar and more threatening appears the wilderness outside, and more and more courage is needed to venture past the armed guards and beyond the reach of the electronic surveillance network. Voluntary ghettos share with the genuine ones an awesome capacity for letting their isolation self-perpetuate and self-exacerbate. In Richard Sennett's words,[46]

> the cries for law and order are greatest when communities are most isolated from other people in the city . . . Cities in America during the past two decades have grown in such a way that ethnic areas have become relatively homogeneous; it appears no accident that the fear of the outsider

has also grown to the extent that these ethnic communities
have been cut off.

Channelling the emotions generated by existential
uncertainty into a frantic search for 'safety-in-community'
acts as all other self-fulfilling prophecies do: once
embarked on, it tends to substantiate its original motives
and produce ever new 'good reasons' and justifications for
the original move. In short, it retrospectively inserts heav-
ier substance into the reasons which triggered it and turns
out ever growing supplies of convincing causes for its
continuation. In the end, its continuation becomes the
proof of its own correctness and cogency – the only proof
that by now it needs.

Let us not be fooled, though, by the apparent common-
ality of the 'safety-in-community' urges; it glosses over
profound differences in socially shaped life conditions.
Even if one forgets for a moment the difference between
the perfumed luxury of the 'quasi-ghettos' and the fetid
squalor of the real ones and imagines that their respective
residents may feel similarly safe when inside, a world of
difference will still remain between (to deploy Max
Weber's famous metaphor) wearing a 'light cloak' and
finding oneself locked in a 'steel casing'. The people who
wear the cloak may find it pretty, cosy and comfortable,
may never go without it and refuse to exchange it for
anything else, but the belief that they can take the cloak
off is what makes it feel like the 'light cloak' it is, never
irritating or oppressive. It is the 'no alternative' situation,
the no-exit fate of the ghetto dweller which makes the
'safety of sameness' feel like a steel casing – tight, cumbersome, incapacitating and impossible to get rid of. It is that
absence of choice in a world of free choosers that is no
less, often more, detested and resented than the drabness
and shabbiness of the unchosen residence. The choosers

of the ghetto-like gated communities may experience their 'safety of sameness' as home; people confined to the real ghettos live in prisons.

In another report from his series of eye-opening ghetto studies, Loïc Wacquant[47] lays bare the 'institutional logics of segregation and aggregation' which result 'in pronouncedly higher levels of blight, poverty and hardship in the ghetto'. Real ghettos may differ between themselves. The American black ghettos, as already noted, are the sedimentation of a double rejection, combining class and race – and skin colour keeps the ghetto residents inside their prison more firmly than would a whole army of prison guards. On the other hand, the French *banlieues* or *cités*, working-class areas with a large immigrant intake, have a racially mixed population and their youngsters fill empty time travelling to the affluent middle-class areas of the city where they can at least hang around for a while in the shopping malls and other favourite haunts of 'ordinary people's' enjoyment. In neither the black ghettos nor the French *cités*, however, is it possible to shake off 'the powerful territorial stigma that attaches to residence in an area publicly recognized as a "dumping ground" for poor people, downwardly mobile working-class households and marginal groups of individuals'.

The mechanism of segregation and exclusion may or may be not supplemented and reinforced by additional race/skin colour factors, but ultimately all its varieties are essentially the same:

> to be poor in a rich society entails having the status of a social anomaly and being deprived of control over one's collective representation and identity; the analysis of public taint in the American ghetto and the French urban periphery [shows] the *symbolic dispossession* that turns their inhabitants into veritable social outcasts.

In a nutshell, the ghettoization is an organic part of the waste-disposal mechanism set in motion in times when the poor are no longer of use as a 'reserve army of producers' and have become instead flawed, and for that reason also useless, consumers. The ghetto, as Wacquant sums up his findings, 'serves not as a reservoir of disposable industrial labour but a mere dumping ground for [those for whom] the surrounding society has no economic or political use'.

Ghettoization parallels and complements the criminalization of poverty; there is an ongoing exchange of population between the ghettos and penitentiaries, each serving as a huge and growing input source for the other. Ghettos and prisons are two varieties of the strategy of 'tying the undesirables to the ground', of *confinement* and *immobilization*. In a world in which mobility and the facility to be on the move have become principal factors of social stratification, this is (both physically and symbolically) a weapon of ultimate exclusion and degradation, of the recycling of the 'lower classes' and the poor in general into an 'underclass' – a category that has been cast outside the class or any other social system of functional significance and utility and defined from the start by reference to its endemically criminal proclivities. In another study[48] Wacquant emphasizes the link between the criminalization of poverty and the normalization of precarious wage labour in a 'flexible' labour market. Having withdrawn from its role of norm-setting supervisor of labour relations, and increasingly from its economic function in general, the state resorts instead to pain-inflicting (Neil Christie's description of penal policy relying mostly on prison confinement) as a means of reconciling the poor to their new condition: once they have become the sole alternatives to the uncertainties of a deregulated labour market, prison and the ghetto transform a meek acceptance of the 'casino economy' with its no-rules game of survival into a bearable, perhaps even a desirable, option.

> The same parties, politicians, pundits, and professors who yesterday mobilized, with readily observable success, in support of '*less* government' as concerns the prerogatives of capital and the utilization of labour, are now demanding, with every bit as much fervour, '*more* government' to mask and contain the deleterious social consequences, in the lower regions of social space, of the deregulation of wage labour and the deterioration of social protection.

We may say that the prisons are ghettos with walls, while ghettos are prisons without walls. They differ from each other mostly by the method by which their inmates are held in place and prevented from escaping – but immobilized, barred from escape routes and held firmly in place they are in both cases. Measured against their condition, even a modicum of mobility feels like unbridled freedom, and the steely grip of the 'flexible labourmarket' seems like a benign embrace. Helping others to bear the hardships of a precarious life is the last function which the otherwise useless outcasts, now incarcerated in their ghetto dwellings or prison cells, have been allowed to perform by affluent, consumer, 'liquid modern' society.

That function would be harder to fulfil were the ghetto-dwellers offered, as compensation, that community shelter which the others, thrown into turbulent waters without lifebelts and unattended by lifeguards, dream about in vain. This is not the case, though. Ghetto life does not sediment community. Sharing stigma and public humiliation does not make the sufferers into brothers; it feeds mutual derision, contempt and hatred. A stigmatized person may like or dislike another bearer of stigma, stigmatized individuals may live in peace or be at war with each other – but one thing they are unlikely to do is to develop mutual respect. 'The others like me' means the others as unworthy as I myself have been repeatedly told that I am and been shown to be; 'to be more like them' means to be more unworthy than I already am.

Contemporary sites of forceful and stigmatizing social segregation have inherited their name from the late medieval ghettos – but again the sharing of names conceals more than it reveals. To quote Wacquant again,[49]

> whereas the ghetto in its classical form acted partly as a protective shield against brutal racial exclusion, the hyperghetto has lost its positive role of collective buffer, making it a deadly machinery for naked social relegation.

No 'collective buffer' can be forged in the contemporary ghettos for the single reason that ghetto experience dissolves solidarity and destroys mutual trust before they have been given a chance to take roots. A ghetto is not a greenhouse of community feelings. It is on the contrary a laboratory of social disintegration, atomization and anomie.

> To regain a measure of dignity and reaffirm the legitimacy of their own status in the eyes of society, residents of both *cité* and ghetto typically overstress their moral worth as individuals (or as family members) and join in the dominant discourse of denunciation of those who undeservingly 'profit' from social programmes, *faux pauvres* and 'welfare cheats'. It is as if they could gain value only by devaluing their neighbourhood and their neighbours. They also engage in a variety of strategies of social distinction and withdrawal which converge to undermine neighbourhood cohesion.

To sum up: ghetto means the *impossibility of community*. This feature of the ghetto makes the policy of exclusion embodied in spatial segregation and immobilization a doubly safe, foolproof choice in a society which can no longer keep all its members playing the 'only game in town', but wishes to keep all the rest who can play it busy and happy, and first and foremost obedient.

9

Many Cultures, One Humanity?

'Multiculturalism' is the most common answer given these days by the learned and opinion-making classes to the world's uncertainty about the kinds of values that deserve to be cherished and cultivated, and the directions that should be pursued with rugged determination. That answer is fast becoming the canon of 'political correctness'; more, it turns into an axiom that no longer needs to be spelled out, into the prolegomena to all further deliberation, the cornerstone of *doxa*: not a knowledge itself, but the unthought, tacit assumption of all leading-to-knowledge thinking.

In a nutshell, the invocation of 'multiculturalism' when made by the learned classes, that contemporary incarnation of modern intellectuals, means: *Sorry, we cannot bail you out from the mess you are in.* Yes, there is confusion about values, about the meaning of 'being human', about the right ways of living together; but it is up to you to sort it out in your own fashion and bear the consequences in the event that you are not happy with the results. Yes, there is a cacophony of voices and no tune is likely to be sung in unison, but do not worry: no tune is necessarily better than the next, and if it were there wouldn't at any rate be a way of knowing it – so feel free to sing (compose, if you can) your own tune (you won't add to the cacophony anyway; it is already deafening and one more tune won't change anything).

To his trenchant statement about the fatuity of the 'multiculturalist' creed Russell Jacoby gave the title *The End of Utopia*.[50] There is a message in this title: learned classes of our times have nothing to say about the preferred shape of the human condition. It is for this reason that they seek escape in 'multiculturalism', that 'ideology of the end of ideology'.

To stand up against the status quo always takes courage, considering the awesome forces gathered behind it – and courage is a quality which intellectuals once famous for their obstreperous radicalism have lost on the way to their new roles and 'niches' as experts, academic boffins or media celebrities. One is tempted to take this slightly updated version of *le trahison des clercs* for the explanation of the puzzle of the learned classes' resignation and indifference.

This temptation needs, however, to be resisted. More important reasons than the cold feet of the learned elite stand behind the intellectualists' journey to their present day equanimity. The learned classes have not made the journey alone. They travelled with a lot of company: together with increasingly exterritorial economic powers, with a society increasingly engaging its members in their role of consumers rather than producers, and with increasingly fluid, 'liquidized', 'deregulated' modernity. And they have undergone in the course of that journey similar transformations to those which were the lot of the rest of their fellow-travellers. Among the transformations all the travellers shared, two in particular stand out as plausible explanations of the spectacular career of the 'ideology of the end of ideology'. The first is *disengagement* as the new strategy of power and domination; the second – *excess* as the present-day replacement for normative regulation.

Modern intellectuals used to be people with a mission: the vocation they were assigned and that they took up in earnest was to assist in the 're-rooting of the uprooted' (to use the terms which sociologists currently prefer, in the 're-embedding of the disembedded'). That mission split into two tasks.

The first task was to 'enlighten the people', that is to supply the disoriented and perplexed men and women plucked out from the monotonous routine of communal life with axiological gyroscopes and cognitive frames that would allow each one of them to navigate the unfamiliar and turbulent waters demanding such life skills as they had never before needed and had never had the chance to learn; to put into place new orientation points, new life purposes and new loyalties and new standards of conformity instead of those that used to be provided by the communities in which human lives, from cradle to grave, were inscribed, but which came to be defunct, were no longer accessible or fell fast out of use.

The other task was to assist the job undertaken by the legislators: to design and build new well-structured and mapped settings that would make such navigation possible and effective, and so give shape to the temporarily shapeless 'mass'; to bring about 'social order', or more exactly an 'orderly society'.

Both tasks derived from the same major undertaking of the modern revolution: state-and-nation building – the replacement of a mosaic of local communities by a new tightly integrated system of the nation-state, of the 'imagined society'. And both tasks required a direct, face-to-face confrontation of all its agents – economic, political or spiritual – with the bodies and souls of the objects of the great transformation under way. Building modern industry boiled down to the challenge of replanting producers from the traditional, community-bound routine into another, designed and administered by the factory owners and their hired supervisors. Building the modern state consisted in replacing the old loyalties to the parish, to the neighbourhood community or to the artisan guild by new citizen-style loyalties to the abstract and distant totality of the nation and the laws of the land. The new loyalties, unlike the old and obsolete ones, could not rely on spontaneous and matter-of-factly followed mechanisms of self-reproduction; they had to be carefully designed and painstakingly instilled in a process of organized mass education. The constructing and servicing of the modern order required managers and teachers. The era of state-and-nation-building had to be, and was, a time of direct engagement between the rulers and the ruled.

This is no longer the case; at least it is ever less the case. Ours are times of disengagement. The panoptical model of domination which used surveillance and hour-by-hour monitoring and correcting of the conduct of the dominated as its main strategy is fast being dismantled and is giving way to self-surveillance and self-monitoring by the dominated, as effective in eliciting the 'right' (system-functional) type of behaviour as the old method of domination – only considerably less costly. Instead of marching columns, swarms.

Unlike marching columns, swarms need no sergeants or corporals; swarms find their way unerringly without the offices of the general staff and their marching orders. No one leads a swarm to flowery meadows and no one needs to reprimand and sermonize the sluggards and whip them back into line. Whoever may wish to keep the swarms on target should tend to the flowers in the meadow, not to the trajectory of an individual bee. It is as if the two-hundred-year-old oracle of Claude Saint-Simon and Karl Marx's vision of communism have come true: the management of humans is being replaced by the management of things (with the humans expected to follow the things and adjust their own actions to their logic)

Unlike marching columns, swarms are *coordinated* without being *integrated*. Unlike in a marching column, each of the 'units' which combine into a swarm is a 'voluntary', self-propelling and self-directing entity, but again unlike in a marching column the possible randomness of the overall effects of autonomy is cancelled without resorting to integration-through-obedience-to-command. No command is given, no call to discipline is heard. If appeals are made, they are addressed to 'individual interest' and understanding. The sanction threatening inappropriate conduct is self-inflicted harm, and the harm is blamed on the ignorance of interest – individual interest, not 'the good of the whole'. The swarm can move in a synchronized way without any of its entities having the slightest idea what a 'common good' may mean. Just like the watching towers of the panopticon, those other costly appurtenances of the 'engaged power', ideological indoctrination and mobilization, have become redundant.

According to the version of the great disengagement drama given by Daniel Cohen,[51] Sorbonne economist, it is no longer the function of the enterprise to guide, regulate and control its employees – it is now the other way round: it is up to the employees to prove their mettle, to demonstrate that they bring assets which other employees lack. In a curious reversal of Karl Marx's model of the capitalist–worker relation, where capitalists paid only for the bare minimum necessary for the reproduction of the workers' capacity to work, their 'labour force', but demanded labour far in excess of their expenditure, present-day companies pay employees for the time they are required to work for the company but lay claim to all their capacities, their whole life and total personality. Cutthroat competition moved from outside to inside the company offices: work means daily tests of capability and dedication, accumulated merits do not guarantee future stability. Cohen quotes a report of the National Agency for Work Conditions: 'Frustration, isolation, competition dominate' the condition of the employees. He quotes Alain Ehrenberg:[52] neuroses caused by conflicts with authority figures gave way 'to depressions, caused by the fear of not being "up to the task" and not giving a "performance" as good as that given by the next fellow-employee'. And finally, Robert Linhart:[53] the counterparts of autonomy and the spirit of initiative are 'suffering, disarray, malaise, feelings of helplessness, stress and fear'. With working effort transformed into a daily struggle for survival, who needs supervisors? With the employees whipped in by their own horror of endemic insecurity, who needs managers to crack the whips?

From marching columns to swarms; from classrooms to the media network, internet and learning software ever less distinguishable from computer games. Job-seekers are expected (and relied upon) to 'get on their bikes' or locate a friendly small-business consultant (Gordon Brown, the British Chancellor of the Exchequer, proposed to arm all job-seekers with free mobile telephones, to make sure that they would always be at beck and call); like stocks and currencies, learners are expected (and relied upon) to 'find their own levels'. In neither case is the old-fashioned engagement, that mixture of rigorous supervision and caring wardenship, called for. Whatever management is left means indirect, oblique manipulation-through-seduction: it is a management at-a-distance.

The second seminal departure – the replacement of normative regulation and policing with the seductive powers of excess – is closely related to the transformation of domination strategies and the advent of coordination without integration.

The death sentence on norms was never officially passed, let alone ever reached the headlines, but the fate of the norm was sealed when out of the chrysalis of the capitalist society of producers there emerged (metaphorically speaking) the butterfly of the society of consumers. This metaphor is only partially correct, though, since the passage in question was nowhere near as abrupt as the birth of a butterfly. It took a long time to notice that too much had changed in human life conditions and life purposes for the emergent state of affairs to be viewed as no more than a new and improved version of the old; that the game of life acquired enough new rules and stakes to deserve a name of its own. Retrospectively, however, we can locate the birth of consumer society and consumer mentality roughly in the last quarter of the previous century, when the Smith/Ricardo/Marx/Mill labour theory of value was challenged by the Menger/Jevons/Walras marginal utility theory: when it was said loud and clear that what endows things with value is not the sweat needed to produce them (as Marx would say), or the self-renunciation necessary to obtain them (as Georg Simmel suggested), but a *desire seeking satisfaction*; when the ancient *querelle* as to whether the maker or the user was a better judge of the value of things was resolved in unambiguous terms in favour of the user, and the question of the right to pass competent judgement was blended with the issue of value-authorship rights. Once that happened, it became clear that (as Jean-Joseph Goux put it) 'to create value, all that is necessary is, by whatever means possible, to create a sufficient intensity of desire' and that 'what ultimately creates surplus value is the manipulation of surplus desire.'[54]

Indeed, as Pierre Bourdieu was famously to put it later, temptation and seduction have come to replace normative regulation and obtrusive policing as the principal means of system construction and social integration. It is the norm breaking (or rather the perpetual transcendence of norm, with a haste which denies habits the time they need to congeal into norms) that is the main effect of temptation and the essence of seduction. And in the absence of norm, excess is life's only hope. In a society of producers, excess was equivalent to waste and for that reason resented and preached against; but it was born as a disease of life-towards-norm (a terminal disease, as it transpired). In a world devoid of norms, excess had turned from poison into medicine for life illnesses; perhaps the sole life support available. Excess, that sworn enemy of the norm, has itself become the norm; perhaps the only norm there is. A curious norm to be sure, one escaping all definition. Having broken normative fetters, excess lost its meaning. Nothing is excessive once excess is the norm.

In the words of Jacques Ellul,[55] fear and anguish are nowadays the 'essential characteristics' of 'Western man', rooted as they are in the 'impossibility of reflecting on such an enormous multiplicity of options'. New roads are built and entry blocked to old ones, the inflows, exits and directions of permitted traffic keep changing places, and newly fashionable land-rovers (those on four wheels, and even more so those composed of electric signals) have made of beaten tracks and signposed roads something altogether redundant. The new trade-off makes the wanderers cherish their freedom of movement daily and proudly display their speed and the accelerating power of their vehicles; at night they also dream of more security and self-confidence for when, during the day, they have to decide which turn to take and at what destination to aim.

Heather Höpfl[56] observed a few years ago that the supply of excess is fast turning into the major concern of late modern social life, and coping with excess is what

passes in late modern society for individual freedom – the
only form of freedom known to the men and women of
our times.

> As the end of the 20th century approaches, there is an
> increasing preoccupation with the elaborate production,
> apparently to serve the interests of consumption, and pro-
> liferation of excess, of a promising liberating heterogeneity
> of choice and experience, of the construction and pursuit
> of sublime objects of desire. The construction of sublime
> artefacts, objects of desire, personalities, 'life-styles', styles
> of interaction, ways of acting, ways of constructing identity
> and so on becomes an oppressive drudgery masquerading
> as ever-extending choice. Matter fills up all space. Choice
> is bewildering illusion.

Illusion or not, these are the life conditions into which
we have been cast: the one thing about which there is no
choice. If the sequence of steps is not predetermined by a
norm (let alone by an unambiguous norm), it is only
continuous experimentation that holds out any hope of
ever finding the target, and such experimentation
demands a lot of alternative roads. George Bernard Shaw,
great wit but also a dedicated amateur photographer,
quipped once that like cod who need to spawn myriads of
eggs so that a few offspring can survive to maturity, a
photographer needs to take a myriad of shots so that a
few prints can be of real quality. We all seem to follow the
cod's recipe for survival now. Excess becomes a precept
of reason. Excess does not seem excessive any more, nor
does waste seem wasteful. The prime meaning of the
'excessive' and the 'wasteful' and the prime reason for
resenting them in the sober, coldly calculating mode of
instrumental rationality is, after all, their 'uselessness'; but
in a life of experimentation excess and waste are anything
but useless – they are, indeed, the indispensable con-

ditions of the rational search for ends. When does excess become excessive? When does waste become wasteful? There is no obvious way of answering such questions, and most certainly no way of answering them in advance. One may bewail wasted years and excessive expenditures of energy and money, but one cannot tell the excessive from the right measure nor the waste from the necessity before fingers are singed and the time of regret has arrived.

I suggest that the multiculturalists' 'ideology of the end of ideology' can best be interpreted as an intellectual gloss on the human condition shaped under the twin impacts of power-through-disengagement and regulation-through-excess. 'Multiculturalism' is a way of adjusting the role of the learning classes to these new realities. It is a manifesto for reconciliation: the new realities are surrendered to, not challenged and not contested – let things (human subjects, their choices and the fate which follows them) 'take their own course'. It is also a product of mimicry of a world marked by disengagement as the principal strategy of power and by the substitution of variety and excess for targeted norms. If realities are not questioned and are assumed to allow no alternative, one can render them liveable only by replicating their pattern in one's own fashion of life.

In the new *Weltanschauung* of the opinion-makers and opinion-disseminators, the realities in question are visualized after the pattern of the late medieval God construed by the Franciscans (particularly the Fratricelli, their 'Minor Brothers' fraction) and the Nominalists (most famously, William of Ockham). In Michael Allen Gillespie's summary,[57] that Franciscan/Nominalist God was 'capricious, fearsome in His power, unknowable, unpredictable, unconstrained by nature and reason and indifferent to good and evil'. Above all, He stayed steadfastly beyond the reach of human intellectual powers and pragmatic abilities. Nothing could be gained by efforts to force God's hand – and since all attempts to do so were bound to be in vain and bore testimony to human conceit, they were both sinful and unworthy of trying. God owed nothing to humans. Having stood them on their feet and told them to seek their own ways, He retreated and retired. In the essay 'Dignity of man', Giovanni Pico della Mirandola,[58] the great codifier of the confident ambitions of the Renaissance, drew the sole conclusions that could sensibly be drawn from God's retreat. God, he concluded, made man

> as a creature of undetermined nature, and placing him in the middle of the universe, said this to him: 'Neither an established place, nor a form belonging to you alone, nor any special function have We given to you, O Adam, and that for this reason that you may have and possess, according to your desire and judgment, whatever place, whatever form, and whatever function you shall desire . . . You, who are confined by no limits, shall determine for yourself your own nature . . .

It is society's turn now to follow the example of the Franciscan/Nominalist God and to retire. Peter Drucker, that William of Ockham and Pico della Mirandola of the 'liquid modern' capitalism era rolled into one, summed up the new wisdom, in keeping with the spirit of the age, in a sound-bite: 'No more salvation by society.' It is now up to human individuals to make the case 'according to their desire and judgement', to prove that case and to defend it against the promoters of other cases. There is no point in invoking the verdicts of society (the last of the authorities to which the modern ear agreed to listen) in order to support one's case: first, the invocation won't be believed since the verdicts – if there are any – are unknown and bound to stay unknown; secondly, one thing one knows for sure about society's verdicts is that they would never hold for long and that there is no knowing which way they might turn next; and thirdly, like the God of late medieval times, society is 'indifferent to good and evil'.

It is only when society is assumed to have such a nature that 'multiculturalism' holds water. If 'society' has no preferences apart from the preference that humans, singly or severally, make their own preferences, then there is no way of knowing whether one preference is better than another. Commenting on Charles Taylor's call to accept and respect the differences between communally chosen cultures, Fred Constant[59] observed that following that call has a two-pronged effect: the right to be different is acknowledged, together with the right to *indifference*. Let me add that while the right to difference is granted to others, it is as a rule those who grant such a right who usurp for themselves the right to stay indifferent – to abstain from judgement. When mutual tolerance is coupled with indifference, communal cultures may live alongside each other, but they seldom talk to each other, and if they do they tend to use the barrel of a gun for a telephone. In a world of 'multiculturalism', cultures may coexist but it is hard for them to benefit from a shared life.

Constant asks: is cultural pluralism a value in its own right, or does its value derive from the suggestion (and hope) that it may improve the quality of shared existence? It is not immediately clear which of the two answers the multiculturalist programme prefers; the question is far from being rhetorical, and the choice between answers would need more to be said about what is meant by the 'right to difference'. That right also allows two interpretations, differing starkly in their consequences.

One interpretation implies the solidarity of explorers: while we all, singly or collectively, are embarked on the search for the best form of humanity, since we would all wish eventually to avail ourselves of it, each of us explores a different avenue and brings from the expedition somewhat different findings. None of the findings can *a priori* be declared worthless, and no earnest effort to find the best shape for common humanity can be discarded in advance as misguided and undeserving of sympathetic attention. On the contrary: the variety of findings increases the chance that fewer of the many human possibilities will be overlooked and remain untried. Each finding may benefit all explorers, whichever road they have themselves chosen. It does not mean that all findings are of equal value; but their true value may only be established through a long dialogue, in which all voices are allowed to be heard and bona fide, well-intentioned comparisons can be conducted. In other words, recognition of cultural variety is the beginning, not the end, of the matter; it is but a starting point for a long and perhaps tortuous, but in the end beneficial, *political process*.

A true political process, consisting of dialogue and negotiation and aiming at an agreed resolution, would be preempted and made all but unfeasible if from the start the superiority of some contenders and the inferiority of others were to be assumed. But it would also grind to a halt before it had begun if the second interpretation of cultural plurality were to win the day: namely, if it is assumed (as the 'multiculturalist' programme in its most common version does, overtly or tacitly) that each extant difference is worthy of perpetuation just for being a difference.

Charles Taylor[60] rightly rejects the second possibility:

> a proper respect for equality requires more than a presumption that further study will make us see things this way, but actual judgments of equal worth applied to the customs and creations of these different cultures . . . In this form, the demand for equal recognition is unacceptable.

But then Taylor makes his refusal contingent on the assertion that the question of the relative worth of cultural choices needs to be left to *further study*: 'the last thing one wants at this stage from Eurocentred intellectuals is positive judgments of the worth of cultures that they have not intensively studied.' Recognition of value stays firmly in the intellectuals' offices. And, true to the nature of academic progessions, it would be as wrong as it is bizarre to expect a considered judgement without a 'study project' first designed and then seen through *sine ira et studio*. 'On examination, either we will find something of great value in culture C, or we will not.' It is, however, we the occupants of academic offices who are entitled to call a finding a finding. Taylor reproaches the 'multiculturalistically' predisposed intellectuals for betraying their academic vocation, while he should censure them for shirking the duties of *homo politicus*, member of the *polity*.

Taylor goes on to suggest that in cases when we seem to know that a certain culture is worthy in itself and thus also worthy of perpetuation, no doubt should remain that the difference embodied by a given community needs to be preserved for the future, and so the rights of the individuals currently alive to make such choices as would cast the future of that difference in doubt need to be restrained. By obliging its residents to send their children to francophone schools, Quebec – in no way an exotic and mysterious but a thoroughly studied and known example – provides Taylor with a pattern for what can (or should) be done in such a case:

It is not just the matter of having the French language available to those who might choose it . . . [I]t also involves making sure that there is a community of people here in the future that will want to avail itself of the opportunity to use the French language. Policies aimed at survival actively seek to *create* members of the community, for instance, in their assuring that future generations continue to identify as French-speakers.

Quebec is a 'soft' (one would say, innocuous) case, which makes a supposition of its general value that much easier. The validity of the case would be more difficult to sustain were another token of cultural distinction-cum-separation chosen – one that, unlike the French language (or any other language, for that matter), we, the 'Eurocentred intellectuals', multilingual as we are though otherwise fond of our own habitual fads and foibles, would rather detest and prefer to keep our distance from, hiding behind the not-yet-undertaken or still-unfinished research projects. The generalization would also seem much less convincing if we were to recall that the French language in the case of Quebec is but one and an uncharacteristically benign member of a large family of tokens, most of them considerably more malignant, which tend to be used by communities all over the world to keep living members within the ranks and to 'create new members' (that is, to oblige the newly born of the yet-unborn to stay in the ranks, predetermining by the same token their choices and perpetuating the communal separation); other members of that family are, for instance, female circumcision or ritual head-dresses for schoolchildren. If this is recalled, we may be readier to accept that, as much as we should respect the right of a community to protection against assimilatory or atomizing forces administered by the state or the dominant culture, we must respect the right of individuals to protection against choice-denying or choice-preventing communal pressures. The two rights are notoriously difficult to reconcile and to respect simultaneously, and the question we confront daily and must answer daily is how to proceed when they clash. Which of the two rights is the stronger – strong enough to annul or set aside the demands invoking the other?

Replying to Charles Taylor's interpretation of the right to recognition, Jürgen Habermas[61] brings into the debate another value, the 'democratic constitutional state', largely missing from Taylor's reasoning. If we agree that recognition of cultural variety is the right and proper starting point for all sensible discussion of shared human values, we should also agree that the 'constitutional state' is the sole framework in which such a debate can be conducted. To make clearer what is involved in the notion, I would prefer to speak of 'republic', or following Cornelius Castoriadis, of 'autonomous society'. An autonomous society is inconceivable without the autonomy of its members; a republic is inconceivable without the well-entrenched rights of the individual citizen. This consideration does not necessarily resolve the issue of conflicting community and individual rights, but it does make evident that without democratic practice by free-to-self-assert individuals that issue cannot be dealt with, let alone resolved. The protection of the individual from his or her community's demand for conformity may not be a task 'naturally' superior to that of the community's bid for survival in its separate identity. But the protection of the individual/ citizen of the republic from *both* anti-communal and communal pressures is the preliminary condition of performing any of those tasks.

As Habermas puts it,

A correctly understood theory of rights requires a politics of recognition that protects the integrity of the individual in the life contexts in which his or her identity is formed . . . All that is required is the consistent actualization of the system of rights. There would be little likelihood of this, of course, without social movements and political struggles

> . . . [T]he process of actualizing rights is indeed embedded in contexts that require such discourses as an important component of politics – discussion about a shared conception of the good and a desired form of life that is acknowledged to be authentic.

Universality of citizenship is the preliminary condition of all meaningful 'politics of recognition'. And, let me add, universality of humanity is the horizon by which all politics of recognition, to be meaningful, needs to orient itself. Universality of humanity does not stand in opposition to the pluralism of the forms of human life; but the test of truly universal humanity is its ability to accommodate pluralism and make pluralism serve the cause of humanity – to enable and to encourage 'ongoing discussion about the shared conception of the good'. Such a test can be passed only as the conditions of republican life are met. As Jeffrey Weeks poignantly put it,[62] the argument about common values which we seek requires 'the enhancement of life-chances, and the maximization of human freedom':

> There is no privileged social agent to attain the ends; merely the multiplicity of local struggles against the burden of history and the various forms of domination and subordination. Contingency, not determinism, underlies our complex present.

The vision of indeterminacy is, no doubt, daunting. But it can also mobilize to a greater effort. One possible response to indeterminacy is the 'ideology of the end of ideology' and the practice of disengagement. Another, equally reasonable but much more promising, response is the assumption that at no other time has the keen search for common humanity, and a practice that follows such an assumption, been as imperative and urgent as it is now.

Fred Constant quotes Amin Maalouf, the Franco-Lebanese writer settled in France, on the subject of the reactions of the 'ethnic minorities' or immigrants to the criss-crossing cultural pressures to which they are exposed in the country of arrival. Maalouf's conclusion is that the more the immigrants feel that their original cultural lore is respected in their new home, and the less they feel that because of their different identity they are resented, pushed out, threatened or discriminated against   the more willingly they open up to the cultural offerings of the new country and the less convulsively they hold on to their own separate ways. For the prospects of cross-cultural dialogue, this is a crucial insight. It points once more to what we have often sensed before: to the close relation between the degree of security on the one hand, and the 'defusing' of the issue of cultural plurality, with an overcoming of cultural separation and a willingness to participate in the search for common humanity, on the other.

Insecurity (among the immigrant as much as among the native population) tends to transform multiculturality into 'multicommunitarianism'. Profound or trifling, salient or hardly noticeable cultural differences are used as building materials in the frenzied construction of defensive walls and missile launching pads. 'Culture' becomes a synonym for a besieged fortress, and in fortresses under siege the inhabitants are required to manifest their unswerving loyalty daily and to abstain from any hob-nobbing with outsiders. 'Defence of the community' must take precedence over all other commitments. Sitting at the same table with 'the aliens', rubbing shoulders while visiting the same places, not to mention falling in love and marrying across the community's borders, are signs of treachery and reasons for ostracism and banishment. Communities so constructed become expedients aimed principally at the perpetuation of division, separation, isolation and estrangement.

Security is the enemy of walled-up and fenced-off community. Feeling secure makes the fearsome ocean separating 'us' from 'them' seem more like an inviting swimming pool. The awesome precipice stretching between the community and its neighbours looks more like a gentle and easy roving/roaming/rambling patch full of pleasurable adventures. Understandably, the defenders of communal isolation tend to be nonplussed by symptons showing that the fears haunting the community are dissipating; knowingly or not, they develop vested interests in the enemy guns aimed at the community's walls. The greater the threat, the deeper the insecurity, the more tightly the ranks of the defenders are likely to be locked, and the more likely they are to stay locked for the foreseeable future.

Security is a necessary condition of dialogue between cultures. Without it, there is little chance that communities will open up to each other and engage in a conversation which may enrich them all and enhance the humanity of their togetherness. With it, the prospects for humanity look bright.

The security in question is, however, a wider problem than most advocates of multiculturalism, in tacit (or inadvertent) collusion with the preachers of communal separation, are willing to admit. Narrowing the issue of endemic insecurity to genuine or putative threats to communally sustained uniqueness is a mistake which draws attention away from its true sources. Nowadays, community is sought as a shelter from the gathering tides of global turbulence – tides originating as a rule in faraway places which no locality can control on its own. The sources of the overwhelming feeling of insecurity are sunk deep in the widening gap between the condition of 'individuality *de jure*' and the task of acquiring 'individuality *de facto*'. The construction of walled-up communities does nothing to close that gap, but everything to make closing it more difficult – nay impossible. Instead of aiming at the sources of insecurity, it channels attention and energy away from them. None of the adversaries in the ongoing 'us versus them' war gain in security from it; all, however, are made easier targets, indeed 'sitting ducks', for the globalizing forces – the only forces likely to benefit from suspending the search for common humanity and joint control over the human condition.

Afterword

We miss community because we miss security, a quality crucial to a happy life, but one which the world we inhabit is ever less able to offer and ever more reluctant to promise. But community remains stubbornly missing, eludes our grasp or keeps falling apart, because the way in which this world prompts us to go about fulfilling our dreams of a secure life does not bring us closer to their fulfilment; instead of being mitigated, our insecurity grows as we go, and so we go on dreaming, trying, and failing.

Insecurity affects us all, immersed as we all are in a fluid and unpredictable world of deregulation, flexibility, competitiveness and endemic uncertainty, but each one of us suffers anxiety on our own, as a private problem, an outcome of personal failings and a challenge to our private savoir-faire and agility. We are called, as Ulrich Beck has acidly observed, to seek biographical solutions to systemic contradictions; we look for individual salvation from shared troubles. That strategy is unlikely to bring the results we are after, since it leaves the roots of insecurity intact; moreover, it is precisely this falling back on our individual wits and resources that injects the world with the insecurity we wish to escape.

When through a window of a stationary train in which you are sitting you see the train on the next platform start off, you often believe that it is your train that has started moving. In another case of optical illusion, it is your own self that you believe to be standing out from the turmoil as the sole steady point amidst a volatile world in which all the apparently solid parts keep appearing and disappearing, changing shapes and colours each time you look. Your body and soul have a longer life expectation than anything else in that world; whenever you look for certainty, investing in self-preservation seems to be the wisest bet. And so you tend to seek a remedy for the discomforts of insecurity in a care for safety, that is for the integrity of your body with all its extensions and frontline trenches – your home, your possessions, your neighbourhood. As you do so, you grow suspicious of the others around you, and particularly of the strangers among them, those carriers and embodiments of the unpredicted and unpredictable. Strangers are unsafety incarnate and so they embody by proxy that insecurity which haunts your life. In a bizarre yet perverse way their presence is comforting, even reassuring: the diffuse and scattered fears, difficult to pinpoint and name, now have a tangible target to focus on, you know where the dangers reside and you need no longer take the blows of fate placidly. At long last, there is something you can do.

It is difficult (and in the end demeaning) to worry about threats you cannot name, let alone fight against. The sources of insecurity are hidden from view and do not appear on the maps the newsagents stock, so you can neither locate them precisely nor try to plug them. However, the causes of unsafety, those strange substances you put in your mouth, or the strange humans who enter, uninvited, the familiar streets you walk, are all too visible. They are all, so to speak, within your reach, and you may think that it is in your power to push them back or 'detoxicate'.

No wonder, therefore, that except for the writers of scholarly books and a few politicians (as a rule politicians not currently in power), you hear little about 'existential insecurity' or 'ontological uncertainty'. Instead, you hear a lot and from everywhere about the threats to the safety of streets, homes and bodies, and what you hear about them seems to chime well with your own daily experience, with the things you see with your own eyes. The demand to cleanse the food we eat from harmful and potentially lethal ingredients and the demand to clear the streets we walk of inscrutable and potentially lethal strangers are the ones most commonly heard when the ways to improve our lives are talked about, and also the ones that feel more credible, indeed self-evident, than any other. Acting in a way that contradicts these demands is what we are most eager to classify as crime and want to be punished, the more severely the better.

Antoine Garapon, a French legal scholar, has observed that while the wicked deeds committed 'at the top', inside the offices of big supranational corporations, stay as a rule out of sight – and if they appear, fleetingly, in public view are poorly comprehended and paid little attention – public wrath is as its most vicious and vengeful when it comes to harm done to human bodies. *Tabagisme* (the French name for tobacco addiction), sexual offences and speeding, the three offences most eagerly condemned by public opinion and for which tougher punishment is demanded, are united by nothing other than the fears about bodily safety. Philippe Cohen, in his widely acclaimed challenge to political elites in a book appropriately titled *Protéger ou disparaître* (Protect or go away), names 'urban violence' among the three major causes of anxiety and unhappiness (alongside unemployment and unsecured old age). As far as public perception is concerned, the belief that urban life is fraught with dangers and that cleansing the streets of obtrusive and peril-auguring strangers is the most urgent of the measures aimed at restoring the missing security appears as a self-evident truth that needs no proof and admits no argument.

In his powerful inquiry into the meaning of 'living together' in the contemporary city, Henning Bech points out that since the cities in which most of us live nowadays are 'large, dense and permanent clusters of heterogeneous human beings in circulation', places in which one is bound to mill in an 'everchanging large crowd of varied strangers moving among one another', we tend to 'become *surfaces* to each other – for the simple reason that this is the only thing a person can notice in the urban space of lots of strangers'. What we see 'on the surface' is the sole available measure by which to evaluate a stranger. What we see may promise pleasure, but it may also portend danger; when it is but surfaces that meet (and always 'in passing'), there is little chance of negotiating and finding out which is which. And the art of living in a crowd of strangers prevents such a chance from materializing – stopping the encounter short of soaking beneath the surface is its most common stratagem.

In our civilized times we do without branding, badges of infamy or dunces' hats to warn us when and from whom to keep our distance, but we have a lot of substitutes to do just that. Surfaces are spattered with them all over – there are too many of them to make sure that we can read them all. As the urban crowd becomes ever more variegated, the chances of coming across modern equivalents of burned-in brands grow accordingly; and the suspicion grows as well that we may be too slow or inept to read out the messages the unfamiliar sights may contain. So we have reasons to be afraid, and then it is only one small step that needs to be made to project our fears on to the strangers that triggered them, and to blame city life for being dangerous: being dangerous because of its variety.

If only the city could be cleansed of the variety that is too rich and extensive to assimilate and feel safe in, while leaving enough variety intact to keep city life as exhilarating and as full of pleasant adventures as it has been – to save some of that spice of life which we, the moderns, would hardly be able to do without . . . Like the desire to have a cake and eat it, these two wishes are at cross-purposes. And yet the most popular (and most seductive) varieties of communitarian projects promise to fulfil both in one go. It is for that reason that they themselves are unfulfillable.

The attraction of the community of communitarian dreams rests on the promise of simplification: brought to its logical limit, simplification means a lot of sameness and a bare minimum of variety. The simplification on offer can only be attained by the separation of differences: by reducing the probability of their meeting and narrowing the extent of communication. This kind of communal unity rests on division, segregation and keeping of distance. These are the virtues figuring most prominently in the advertising leaflets of communitarian shelters.

Given that insecurity, mediated by the channelling of anxiety into safety concerns, was the prime cause of the ailment for which communitarianism was to be a remedy – the community of the communitarian project may only exacerbate the condition it promised to rectify. And it will do so through injecting more potency into the atomizing pressures that were, and continue to be, insecurity's most abundant source. This kind of communitarian idea is also guilty of endorsing and sanctioning the choice of safety as the site on which the major troops of dissent should be deployed and the decisive battle against insecurity staged – and so of cooperating in the channelling of public concerns away from the primary sources of contemporary anxiety.

In the course of this kind of articulation of the purpose and function of community, the other aspects of community missing from contemporary life (the ones directly relevant to the sources of present troubles) tend to be left unthematized and off the agenda. The two tasks which should be invoked by community to counter head-on the pathologies of the atomized society of today on a battleground that truly counts are equality of the resources necessary to recast the fate of individuals *de jure* into the capacities of individuals *de facto*, and collective insurance against individual incapacities and misfortunes. The valour of the original community lay in these two intentions whatever its other demerits might be. The *pensée unique* of our deregulated market society forgoes these tasks and openly proclaims them to be counterproductive – but the preachers of community, ostensibly the sworn adversaries of this kind of society, are reluctant to rally in defence of abandoned tasks.

We are all interdependent in this fast globalizing world of ours, and due to this interdependence none of us can be the master of our fate on our own. There are tasks which each individual confronts but which cannot be tackled and dealt with individually. Whatever separates us and prompts us to keep our distance from each other, to draw boundaries and build barricades, makes the handling of such tasks yet more difficult. We all need to gain control over the conditions under which we struggle with the challenges of life – but for most of us such control can be gained only *collectively*.

Here, in the performance of such tasks, community is most missed; but here as well, for a change, lies community's chance to stop being *missing*. If there is to be a community in the world of the individuals, it can only be (and it needs to be) a community woven together from sharing and mutual care; a community of concern and responsibility for the equal right to be human and the equal ability to act on that right.

Notes

1 Ferdinand Tönnies, *Community and Society*, trans. Charles P. Loomis (New York: Harper, 1963), pp. 47, 65, 49.
2 Robert Redfield, *The Little Community*, and *Peasant Society and Culture* (Chicago: University of Chicago Press, 1971), pp. 4ff.
3 Eric Hobsbawm, *The Age of Extremes* (London: Michael Joseph, 1994), p. 428.
4 Eric Hobsbawm, 'The cult of identity politics', *New Left Review* 217 (1996), p. 40.
5 Jock Young, *The Exclusive Society* (London: Sage, 1999), p. 164.
6 Jonathan Friedman, 'The hybridization of roots and the abhorrence of the bush', in Mike Featherstone and Scott Lash (eds), *Spaces of Culture* (London: Sage, 1999), p. 241.
7 Stuart Hall, 'Who needs "identity"?', in Stuart Hall and Paul du Gay (eds), *Questions of Cultural Identity* (London: Sage, 1996), p. 1.
8 Walter Benjamin, *Illuminations*, ed. Hannah Arendt (New York: Schocken, 1969), p. 257.
9 Jean-Paul Fitoussi and Pierre Rosanvallon, *Le nouvel âge des inégalités* (Paris: Seuil, 1996), p. 32.
10 Sigmund Freud, *The Future of an Illusion*, trans. W. D. Robson-Scott (London: Hogarth Press, 1973), pp. 3–6.
11 Thorstein Veblen, *The Theory of the Leisure Class: an Economic Study of Institutions* (New York: Random House, n.d.), pp. 15, 93.

12   John Stuart Mill, *Principles of Political Economy*, vol. 4 (London: John W. Parker and Son, n.d.), ch. 7.

13   John Foster, *Class Struggle and the Industrial Revolution* (London: Weidenfeld and Nicolson, 1974), p. 33.

14   Richard Sennett, *The Corrosion of Character: the Personal Consequences of Work in the New Capitalism* (New York: Norton, 1998), pp. 42–3.

15   Ibid., p. 45

16   Ibid., pp. 20–1.

17   Maurice R. Stein, *The Eclipse of Community: an Interpretation of American Studies*, 2nd edn (New York: Harper and Row, 1965), p. 329.

18   Richard Rorty, *Achieving Our Country, Leftist Thought in Twentieth-Century America* (Cambridge: Harvard University Press, 1998), pp. 86–7.

19   Dick Pountain and David Robins, 'Too cool to care', extract from a forthcoming book *Cool Rules: Anatomy of an Attitude*, quoted after *The Editor*, 11 Feb. 2000, pp. 12–13.

20   Søren Kierkegaard, *Either/Or*, trans. David F. Swenson and Lillian Marvin Swenson (Princeton: Princeton University Press, 1994); here quoted after David L. Norton and Mary F. Kille (eds), *Philosophies of Love* (Totowa: Helix Books, 1971), pp. 45–8.

21   'The Cultural Globalization Project', *Insight* (Spring 2000), pp. 3–5.

22   Geoff Dench, *Minorities in the Open Society: Prisoners of Ambivalence* (London: Routledge and Kegan Paul, 1986), ch. 10.

23   Ulrich Beck, *World Risk Society* (Cambridge: Polity Press, 1999), p. 2.

24   Rorty, *Achieving Our Country*, pp. 76–7, 79, 83.

25   Ivan Klima, *Between Security and Insecurity*, trans. Gerry Turner (London: Thames and Hudson, 1999), pp. 20, 27–8, 44.

26   Émile Durkheim, *Les règles de la méthode sociologique*, 11th edn (1950), p. 122, here quoted in Anthony Giddens's translation, *Emile Durkheim: Selected Writings* (Cambridge: Cambridge University Press, 1972), p. 100.

27 Friedman, 'The hybridization of roots and the abhorrence of the bush', pp. 239, 241.

28 Nancy Fraser, 'Social justice in the age of identity politics: redistribution, recognition, and participation', in Detlev Claussen and Michael Werz (eds), *Kritische Theorie der Gegenwart* (Hanover: Institut für Soziologie an der Universität Hannover, 1999), pp. 37–60.

29 See Bruno Latour, 'Ein Ding ist ein Thing', *Concepts and Transformations* 1–2 (1998), pp. 97–111.

30 Cornelius Castoriadis, 'Done and to be done', in *Castoriadis Reader*, trans. David Ames Curtis (Oxford: Blackwell, 1997), pp. 400, 414, 397–8.

31 Harvie Ferguson, *The Science of Pleasure* (London: Routledge, 1990), pp. 199, 247.

32 Jacques Ellul, *Métamorphose du bourgeois* (Paris: La Table Ronde, 1998), pp. 81, 91, 94.

33 Max Weber, *Theory of Social and Economic Organization* (part 1 of *Wirtschaft und Gesellschaft*, trans. A. R. Henderson and Talcott Parsons; here quoted after *Max Weber: the Interpretation of Social Reality*, ed. J. E. T. Eldridge (London: Nelson, 1971), pp. 87, 90.

34 Loïc Wacquant, *Les Prisons de la misère* (Paris: Raisons d'Agir, 1999), p. 70.

35 Rorty, *Achieving Our Country*, pp. 83–4.

36 Dench, *Minorities in the Open Society*, pp. 23–6, 156, 184.

37 Jeffrey Weeks, *Making Sexual History* (Cambridge: Polity Press, 2000), pp. 182, 240–3.

38 Saskia Sassen, 'The excesses of globalization and the feminization of survival', *Parallax* (Jan. 2001).

39 Geoff Dench, *Maltese in London: a Case-Study in the Erosion of Ethnic Consciousness* (London: Routledge and Kegan Paul, 1975), pp. 158–9.

40 Rorty, *Achieving Our Country*, p. 88.

41 Alain Touraine, 'Faux et vrais problèmes', in *Une Société fragmentée? Le multiculturalisme en débat* (Paris: La Découverte, 1997).

42 See Paul Virilio, *Polar Inertia*, trans. Patrick Camiller (London: Sage, 1999).

43   Richard Sennett, 'Growth and failure: the new political economy and its culture', in Mike Featherstone and Scott Lash (eds), *Spaces of Culture: City-Nation-World* (London: Sage, 1999), p. 15.

44   Sharon Zukin, *The Culture of Cities* (Oxford: Blackwell, 1995), pp. 39, 38.

45   Loïc Wacquant, ' "A black city within the white"; revisiting America's dark ghetto', *Black Renaissance* 2.1 (Fall/Winter 1998), pp. 141–51.

46   Richard Sennett, *The Uses of Disorder: Personal Identity and City Life* (London: Faber, 1996), p. 194.

47   Loïc J. D. Wacquant, 'Urban outcasts: stigma and division in the black American ghetto and the French urban periphery', *International Journal of Urban and Regional Research* 17.3 (1993), pp. 365–83.

48   Loïc J. D. Wacquant, 'Elias in the dark ghetto', *Amsterdam Sociologisch Tijdschrift* 24.3–4 (1997), pp. 340–9.

49   Loïc Wacquant, 'How penal common sense comes to Europeans: notes on the transatlantic discussion of the neoliberal *doxa*', *European Societies* 1.3 (1999, pp. 319–52.

50   See Russell Jacoby, *The End of Utopia: Politics and Culture in an Age of Apathy* (New York: Basic Books, 1999).

51   Daniel Cohen, *Nos temps modernes* (Paris: Flammarion, 1999), pp. 56, 60–1.

52   Alain Ehrenberg, *La fatigue d'être* (Paris: Odile Jacob, 1998).

53   Robert Linhart, 'L'évolution de l'organisation de travail', in Jacques Kergouat et al. (eds), *Le monde du travail* (Paris: La Découverte, 1998).

54   Jean-Joseph Goux, *Symbolic Economies: After Marx and Freud*, trans. Jennifer Curtiss Gage (Ithaca: Cornell University Press, 1990), pp. 200, 202.

55   Ellul, *Métamorphose du bourgeois*, p. 277.

56   Heather Höpfl, 'The melancholy of the black widow', in Kevin Hetherington and Rolland Munro (eds), *Ideas of Difference* (Oxford: Blackwell, 1997), pp. 236–7.

57   Michael Allen Gillespie, 'The theological origins of modernity', *Critical Review* 13.1–2 (1999), pp. 1–30.

58   *Portable Renaissance Reader*, ed. James Bruce Ross and Mary Martin McLoughlin (New York: Viking, 1953), p. 478.
59   Fred Constant, *Le multiculturalisme* (Paris: Flammarion, 2000), pp. 89–94.
60   Charles Taylor, 'The policy of recognition', in Amy Gutman (ed.), *Multiculturalism* (Princeton: Princeton University Press, 1994), pp. 98–9, 88–9.
61   Jürgen Habermas, 'Struggles for recognition in the democratic constitutional regime', in Gutman, *Multiculturalism*, pp. 125, 113.
62   Jeffrey Weeks, 'Rediscovering values', in Judith Squires (ed.), *Principled Positions* (London: Lawrence and Wishart, 1993), pp. 208–9.

Index